Changing Conversations
for a
Changing World

Fifteen Global Consultants, Coaches, and Leaders
Share Their Stories in Applying
Conversational Intelligence®
to Our Business and Personal Lives

Compiled by the European C-IQ Collective

the three
tomatoes
The Three Tomatoes Book Publishing

Published August 2020
Printed in North America and Europe

ISBN: 978-1-7353585-2-9

For information address:

The Three Tomatoes Book Publishing
6 Soundview Rd.
Glen Cove, NY 11542
www.thethreetomatoesopublishing.com

Cover design: Susan Herbst

Cover image: iStock Photo

Changing Conversations
for a
Changing World

Fifteen Global Consultants, Coaches, and Leaders
Share Their Stories in Applying
Conversational Intelligence®
to Our Business and Personal Lives

DEDICATION

This book is dedicated to our mentor, coach, and friend,
Judith E. Glaser.

Martin —
Grow forward!
Am proud of you
leadership development.

Jua

FOREWORD

It is an honor for me to be associated with these wonderful consultants, coaches, and authors of *Changing Conversations for a Changing World,* all of whom embody Judith's work.

Judith once said, "When it comes to growing your business, navigating the future is a wiser strategy than working on fixing the past. We have been trained to 'fix problems' and success will follow. Well, this is not true in the world of rapid change."

These chapters exemplify navigating the future in a myriad of challenges in the world of change we have never experienced before. These consultants and coaches are at the forefront of demonstrating how Conversational Intelligence® (C-IQ) can improve not just individual success but the success of entire companies.

Angela Ahrendts, previously the senior vice president of Retail at Apple Inc. and the past CEO of Burberry, said at Judith's funeral, we must "realize how words create worlds, where we are reminded to create shared meaning, separate opinions from facts, and be willing to change our beliefs, while being elegantly inclusive. Her deep thinking on We Centered leadership was so ahead of its time and is one of her greatest contributions to business cultures and society."

I could not be in better company than with the members of the European C-IQ Collective. I wish I could hug you all.

Richard D. Glaser, Ph.D.
Cofounder
The CreatingWE Institute
www.creatingwe.com

CONTENTS

Introduction   P 1

1 Inner Climate Importance in Times of Outer Climate   P 3
  Danger

2 Create Your Own "Yellow Brick Road" to Greatness   P 21

3 Case History: Curiosity, Intentional Listening, and   P 27
  Letting Go

4 Moving from "Stuck" to Lasting Change   P 37

5 Case Study: Navigating Personal Transformation   P 47

6 Transparency as a Catalyst for a Healthy and Sustainable   P 59
  Culture

7 How to Transform Company Culture and Create   P 77
  Engagement

8 Case Study: Agile Project Room   P 95

9 How TRUST Makes for a Safer World   P 107

10 Case Study: Co-creation in Practice   P 123

11 Intuition and Communication A Winning   P 131
     Combination

12 Case Study: Building Trust and a "Power-With" Culture   P143

13 Stress Never Killed Anyone. Did It?   P 153

14 Case Study: Helping Clients' Dreams Come True with   P 165
     the C-IQ Toolbox

15 Inclusion and the Brain   P 171

16 In Memory of My Dearest Friend, Mentor, Colleague   P 187
     Judith E. Glaser

     Biographies   P 197

INTRODUCTION

"Conversations are the golden threads that keep us
connected to others."
~ Judith E. Glaser

How many of you have personally encountered another human being who shifts the tide of the universe? Yes, we know these people exist—Mahatma Gandhi, Martin Luther King, Jr., Mother Teresa—to name a notable few. Some are well recognized and documented in history. Others, like Judith E. Glaser, humbly moved mountains in organizations and beyond just by the way she spoke, the words she used, and the questions she asked. She had a gift to create simultaneously atmospheres of curiosity and acceptance, positivity and connection. Just a few moments with her and your oxytocin elevated to such levels that the world seemed filled with possibilities.

Globally, hundreds of organizational consultants, coaches, and leaders benefitted from three years of education and certification, as Judith joyfully shared her life's work with us, prior to her death in 2018. Throughout our education we learned in smaller groups, often connected across the globe. We juggled time zones, cultures, and varied languages. We learned to listen, ask questions to which we had no answers, and check for understanding. Out of this learning emerged what is known today as the European C-IQ (Conversational Intelligence®) Collective, from which the authors of this book come.

What will you gain from reading this book? As leaders of all levels in companies large and small, you will learn the elements and benefits of creating an agile workspace. You will read about the unbridled freedom that comes with vulnerable self-reflection, a necessity for any leader. You will walk through an authentic story of our own C-IQ coaches' struggle with team co-creation, perceived exclusion, conflict, and the transparent conversations that lead to heightened trust and resolution. Do you desire a culture change in your organization? We have a chapter on that, too…and a chapter about the impact of trust in creating a culture of safety in high reliability organizations, and a chapter about stress and the brain.

Diverse perspectives, cultures, and experiences of multiple authors across Europe and the U.S. have come together to form this eclectic collection of stories. The golden thread that binds us together is Judith. Her legacy to bridge healthful and co-creative connections by changing the way we converse with one another comes to you, through the Collective's eyes.

Wishing you many golden threads of insights and connections.
Warmly,

The European C-IQ Collective

1

Inner Climate Importance in Times of Outer Climate Danger

By Carina Vinberg
Leadership Trainer | Group Developer | Coach
Stockholm, Sweden

Two women, one dog, no electricity or running water, nine months in a trapper's cabin, three months in total darkness.
This is **Hearts in the Ice.**

- What is the temperature like in the Arctic at 78th longitude?
- What is the temperature like in your insides when a polar bear drops in for a visit?
- What to do when you have run out of coffee 140 kilometers away from civilization?

When you meet the Queen of the Arctic (female polar bear), when you have decided to live your dream at 78th longitude, success is about communication, values, self-leadership and deep gratitude.

Hearts in the Ice was initiated by two Norwegian women, Hilde and Sunniva, determined to live their dream in the Arctic and bring awareness around climate change to the global community. They worked on their projects that involved collecting data for global scientists studying climate change, northern lights, plastic waste in oceans, cloud formations, the sea, permafrost, and wildlife. All projects are geared toward better understanding of the impact of climate change.

Hilde and Sunniva
Photo Credit: Hearts in the Ice

My goal was to prepare and support these two extraordinary women in achieving their goal of sustaining fortitude and perseverance during the upcoming winter months in arctic temperatures.

This story is about two fearless and adventurous women, whom I coached and trained in preparation for their extended sojourn in a trapper's cabin located in Bamsebu, about 140 kilometers from Longyearbyen in the Arctic Circle. The cabin was originally built for whalers in 1930. We had a clearly defined process in place, ranging from what tools would be needed to the development of self-leadership strategies, and how to navigate communication challenges that could arise during their isolation from the outside world.

During the winter months, when the fjords freeze over, the cabin can only be reached by snowmobile or dogsled. In summer, Bamsebu is accessible only by boat— weather permitting.

How It All Began

I am a leadership trainer and coach working with individuals, executives, teams, and organizations, as well as with top athletes. My passion lies in exploring values and core competencies in order to foster self-leadership. I bring my whole self to my work with focus and engagement. My strengths include a great amount of curiosity, energy, and generosity.

I have acquired an extensive repertoire of communication tools that I adapt to a given situation to build trust, partnering, and mutual respect.

The most important "tools" are the participants themselves, with whom I use storytelling and listening which then lead to new meanings and self-reflection.

In May 2018, I joined an expedition on board a Norwegian ship, from the mainland of Norway via Bear Island to Longyearbyen, Svalbard with Johanna Stålnacke, a mountaineering guide.

Johanna and I had worked together over the past five years to mentally prepare her for her entry exam and certification to become an International Mountaineering Guide. This is an extremely tough undertaking. We worked on self-leadership and how to mindfully handle the challenges faced while climbing and skiing the mountains. We pivoted toward the positive and possible, envisioning rain giving way to sunshine and slippery stones turning to stones that offered grip. Most of all, how to hold on to and never lose focus. The right focus!

On board the *Nordstjernan,* an old Hurtigruten ship from the 1950s, we had inspiring conversations about nature and life on Svalbard that included the history of this magical place. Hilde, who was the expedition leader of this trip with sixty participants, came up to me after Johanna and I had given a spontaneous talk on our collaboration.

After hearing our talk, Hilde said, "I would like to have your business card, Carina. I am involved in a project called Hearts in the Ice, and I will get in contact with you."
Said and done. In August, Hilde sent me an email and here we are.

Hilde and Sunniva asked me to help them prepare for this adventure. They thought my experience with helping people explore and identify values and core competencies would be of great value.

As a leadership trainer, supporting and coaching these two women along the way has been an adventure in itself. When two strong leaders begin working together, what is most important?

To begin with, conversations and clarity, getting things done efficiently, and working out how to put pieces of this puzzle together. A puzzle that kept evolving as the time for departure drew closer.

Clarity makes it easier to prioritize and come to decisions. It's also crucial for leadership and credibility. It is vital to be able to decide quickly and accurately if, for example, a polar bear comes knocking at your door. And if that is not enough adrenaline, realizing that six or seven unpredictable young polar bears have settled in next door to you will provide the necessary punch! Being aware of the challenges posed for a two-woman team in a twenty-square-meter space for nine months, three of them in total darkness, without running water or electricity is not to be underestimated!

Awareness of the unaware and unexpected is important in life in general and especially in the Arctic.

Preparing for Bamsebu

Besides working full-time, Hilde and Sunniva had to arrange all the details of the project, including food supplies, planning for more than a hundred people for a send-off trip, social media, sponsorship, and the seven research projects, as well as all the extra equipment and supplies needed for the winter months.

Two women alone in the high Arctic of Svalbard during the harsh winter months is a first. Together they designed, planned, and lived this unique project.

As I worked with Sunniva and Hilde for an entire year before the journey began in 2019, they shared stories about their role models and the qualities they stood for: What about their strengths and the way they lived their lives made them role models? Why was this important to them? And how did they impact their lives?

While sharing stories, they connected on a deeper level. Today Hilde and Sunniva are role models in the global community, sharing their knowledge, inspiration, and wisdom around climate change and continually growing their network of support.

I also helped them with value assessment using Value.Online*.

They ranked personal values that generate an overview map. The outcome showed that both values and storytelling are important because they lead to new insights and awareness.

Why Work with Values?

The tool I use, Value.Online, facilitates the process of emerging our stories and connecting to one another as colleagues at work or as a co-creative team of two, as in the case of Hilde and Sunniva.

We had already started with assessing their personal values and next began sharing and telling *why* a value is important. This is a unique, interactive tool. You simply rank what is most important to you right now. This generates an instant overview map of which values stand out and are most important to you.

Step 1 is Rank, Step 2 is Map, and Step 3 is Act.

Two Different Types of Values

Value.Online has chosen to distinguish between normative and personal values. It gives us the opportunity to work with these two aspects separately. Normative values are the rules and agreements we have in families and in society to be able to agree, while personal, descriptive values tell us what is important to us, what drives us, what we dream of. These personal values evolve and change throughout life.

Knowing yourself is a lifelong project. Ask yourself what your values are, what you stand for, and why something is important to you. In order to work effectively as a team, you need to share and create new stories.

Sunniva and Hilde said that doing this work together gave them permission to think differently. "We live in a world where we all feel guilty for not having or doing enough." They shared that one of the most important things I did for them was to hold them accountable, not only to themselves but to each other: "This could not have happened without the work we did together on assessing values."

Another very important outcome of this work was that, in spite of living together under stressful and even scary conditions, they knew they could trust each other.

I aspired to contribute to building a culture of trust for greater well-being, smooth cooperation, and, ultimately, success. It was important to me to help them create awareness around value-based self-leadership and offer tools to put learning and reflection into practice.

The week before Christmas 2018, I went to meet Hilde and Sunniva in Svalbard to continue the work we had started in October. Finally, I got to meet Sunniva, who flew in from Canada where she lives.

As they began growing together as a team of two, I stepped back so that they could make the most of their time together. This made me creative. For example, I used the few minutes we had in the car driving to the gym to ask them many questions. When preparing breakfast, I turned the breakfast eggs I was boiling into useful metaphors to talk about strengthening our muscles in both body and mind to prepare for upcoming challenges (the hard-boiled egg symbolizing strength as opposed to the raw egg, symbolizing an untrained mind and lack of stamina).

My training and coaching are based on a sound knowledge of neuroplasticity and the latest brain research. We need to understand that as human beings we are made up of biological systems, functions, and needs to understand.

In her book *Conversational Intelligence* (1), Judith E. Glaser describes the Conversational Essentials, that I found to be integral to my coaching work.

These included understanding the impact of and applying:

- Asking questions for which you have no answers
- Double-Clicking (Are we talking about the same thing? Do we have the same agenda?)
- Listening to connect (Show that you really are listening, for example by being attuned to body language.)
- Applying conversational agility. Listening to understand instead of proving ourselves right.

I worked with Sunniva and Hilde to build a framework based on Judith's body of work. The framework presents were extremely helpful in understanding the kind of conversations that trigger the lower, more primitive brain, and which conversations activate higher-level intelligences where trust, integrity, empathy, and good judgment live.

Judith goes on to explain that nine of ten conversations, (2) Benchmark Communication®, Inc and Creating WE® Institute miss the mark. We are addicted to being right, shut down our listening, and end up talking past each other.

Once these tools become embodied as a way of creating meaningful conversations, we begin to connect on a deeper and trust-based level.

We also discussed how neuroscience impacts different parts of the brain depending on whether we are in stress or safety mode. Most notable are cortisol, also known as the stress hormone, that resides in the body for twenty-six hours. Oxytocin, the bonding hormone, floods the body when we feel relaxed and safe. These tools are extremely helpful in understanding how we can Up-Regulate or Down-Regulate behaviors to create inner balance.

Conversational Intelligence offers a framework that helps to connect, navigate conversational nuances, and co-create. Judith shows us how our neural networks are wired to connect and can shift into discovery mode to build trust.

They did not have much time to work with these valuable tools as they had to coordinate meetings, documentary filming, and learning to use the new rifles among many other tasks. This was truly a test of navigating complexity and adapting to each situation as it came our way.

In the Spring of 2019 both women met at the cabin to prepare for their extended stay. They continued sharing stories of their values as they integrated the powerful learning into their everyday lives. When we share stories about our values, relationships are built, and trust can thrive. A solid foundation for cooperation, teamwork, and well-being was laid.

It's easy to believe that you really know each other just because you have been in contact for four years, have shared share polar interests and life dreams.

In many workplaces, people have worked for years together—how many of them can honestly say that they really, really know each other on a deeper level?

For Hilde and Sunniva this has been very important for strengthening their foundation as individuals, growing together as a team, and understanding the importance of living one's values. The *why* surfaced during the storytelling and was integral to their awareness.

Both agreed that had they not had the space to share their stories, they would not have come together in the same way.

Another powerful awareness exercise is Life Journey. You draw a timeline on a piece of paper and map people and events in your life including both the positive and negative aspects that had an important influence. By recounting the past events in this way, long-forgotten stories are surfaced.

By sharing them with another person, often a new perspective emerges. It was difficult to actually find words to describe the insights that both came to—the important part is that they grew closer as colleagues and friends as a result.

Research shows that people who have insight and knowledge of their own personal values are more committed and motivated—both in their private life and at work. If you can also find coherence between your own values and the values in the workplace, the effect is even greater. Stress and anxiety associated with work is reduced. Leaders who have insight into both their personal and organizational values are perceived to be more credible and they find it easier to make decisions. Awareness of personal values can increase engagement at work by up to almost 30 percent.

Stress Creates Another Version of WE

The pace began to accelerate as Hilde and Sunniva tackled all the tasks that needed to be completed before departure. They had to let go of things and prioritize. During the spring months their lives were packed with transatlantic travel, giving speeches, and fundraising interviews, all on top of their full-time jobs at Hurtigruten (Hilde) and Polar Latitudes (Sunniva). Life became a hub filled with stress, decisions that needed to be made on the spot, and high levels of cortisol.

Sufficient sleep and physical training were no longer part of their repertoire. With rising stress levels, it's common to feel irritated and stop listening. The result: miscommunication, mood swings, and apologies.

This was not the way these caring, thoughtful women really wanted to show up. Unfortunately, they were so stressed during the months of preparation that they nearly lost track of their goal. They needed to keep reminding each other of the intention of the whole project. This project would be a life-changing experience for them and worth all the work going into it to realize the dream of a lifetime.

Time for Send-off

Friends, family, sponsors, scientists, press, musicians, TV teams, a total of over a hundred people filled the Hurtigruten boat *Nordstjernan* (the same beautiful old boat I had been on before).

We had a historic trip to Bamsebu. The scientists gave Hilde and Sunniva a crash course on the use of equipment. We all helped to store barrels of food, huge amounts of equipment, and made sure there was fresh water in the tank. The sauna was built in one afternoon, the doghouse for Ettra, the malamute dog, was finished in one day. We sang, ate, cried, and waved goodbye to the three of them—a very touching moment.

It was an amazing send-off for Hilde and Sunniva. A wonderful community of friends, family, scientists, and PR teams expressed their love and appreciation for these two extraordinary women and the adventure they were about to embark upon. It was really lovely to meet and spend time with all on board as well as taking part in the expedition.

Beyond magical: Standing underneath a shower of Aurora
in -32 degrees C
Photo Credit: Hearts in the Ice

The main goal at Bamsebu was to "live the experience." To be fully immersed and live to tell about it. Hilde and Sunniva can proclaim with 100 percent certainty— "We are living it!"

As a coach and communication leader, I encouraged Sunniva and Hilde to keep a daily gratitude journal and appreciate the importance of recording their weekly routines. I asked them to journal every day, regardless of their mood. This exercise was a time to slow down and reflect. They asked themselves, "What am I grateful for today?" For Hilde and Sunniva it could be gratitude for good weather, dry wood, hot coffee, a feast when eating the last two fresh potatoes. Sharing this with each other was also important. "You know, Carina," they said, "when you only have a little you become aware of what you really have."

According to Hilde and Sunniva, the gratitude exercise was like a one-minute meditation where you feel present in the moment by asking:

- What am I grateful for?
- What did I learn today?
- Why?
- Thank you.

Not doing the gratitude book, on the other hand, is like missing out on a daily meditation. Once you start, you wish you had more time. It's that powerful!

I explained to them what happens when the feel-good hormone, oxytocin, kicks in. By expressing gratitude, you are releasing oxytocin throughout the body.

I held them accountable for doing just this, and this has been a crucial factor for their personal development. Through reflection and putting words to experiences, you take a more objective stance, helping to reframe and refocus the event.

Also, the simple act of putting pen to paper activates the brain and creates clarity around both positive and negative aspects. It makes the invisible visible, opens up awareness, and builds trust over time.

"The quality of our culture depends on the quality of our relationships, which depend on the quality of our conversations. Everything happens through conversation!" ~Judith E. Glaser

---

Everything starts with conversation. The more we practice scanning our own system and that of others, we begin to connect in a meaningful way, listen to understand, and "read" the emotional state of the person we engage with. Depending on our mood states, our intent, and the words we use, we either activate higher-level intelligence such as trust, integrity, empathy, and good judgment, or our lower, limbic brain that shuts down good judgment and sends us into a fight, flight, freeze response.

We scheduled monthly check-in calls via satellite connection during the nine-month sojourn at Bamsebu and inquired about any support that might be needed. We decided to meet for either one-to-one coaching sessions or as a group, whatever was needed at the moment. It often ended up being a conversation about what had been on their minds over the past weeks. One of the topics that stood out was their first encounter with a polar bear. This is something we had talked about before the journey. It caused some anxiety, especially as this was an area known for roaming younger and more unpredictable bears. Hilde, having worked at Svalbard for twenty-four years, was not unfamiliar with polar bear encounters, given that she has had at least a hundred encounters with them. Nevertheless, you never know what the next encounter will bring!

Today, polar bears are wandering into inhabited areas in search of food. One dog was killed by a polar bear in Svalbard. Ettra, the malamute, was kept inside the cabin at night. She was also a good source for heat as the ice-cold winter winds were blowing. Plus having a dog around provided a comforting source of oxytocin. Bad moods evaporated when Ettra joined in, tail a-wag.

An agenda for a call looked something like this:

- Checking in. Any challenges? How have you dealt with them?
- Reflective Journal: Explore the progress you have made, reflections.

- Do you see any patterns? Anything you have become aware of?
- Do a "value check."
- Personal coping strategies.
- What have you learned about yourselves and each other during the past months?

Imagine living at the 78th longitude. Getting through a normal day is filled with tasks like attending to the research projects, flying a drone to collect data on the ice, heating the cabin, melting ice for coffee, preparing food, encounters with wildlife, as well as waiting for the right moment to study the skies. Another example of a whole-day activity is washing her hair, Sunniva told me. This is what I would say causes us to slow down, stay mindful and present.

Outside the cabin
Photo credit: Hearts in the Ice

Life Learnings and Learning for Life at the 78th Longitude

Our arctic women have endured dozens of polar bear visits, freezing temperatures, and three months of total darkness and isolation. Covid-19 changed their homecoming plans, so they have decided to repack, restock, and extend their stay to continue citizen science projects and climate change dialogue.

They packed many tools for navigating the wilderness and encounters with wild animals. The other, no less important, tools included mental exercises for self-leadership and teamwork; how to cope with the isolation and the confined living space.

"This has not just been about surviving. Our aim was to thrive and have fun along the way! We have experienced great support in our network, which consists mainly of women leaders from all over the world," they say.

The natural world is our real home. We all need to adopt a different set of values if we are to survive. This is the perfect time to experiment with finding a way to shift mindsets and rethink the way we are living on this beautiful planet.

"Mother Earth Needs Her Daughters!"

The "Arctic women", Hilde and Sunniva, have learned much about themselves through those long days of what is referred to as "Polar Nights." They have danced with their fears and insecurities, which have allowed them to explore their emotions and way of thinking without getting stuck there.

They developed a deep connection to the cycles of life and death around Bamsebu.

"This very connection to the natural world around us brings us to the truth that nothing is permanent and there are no guarantees. It brings us to other truths as well—that life is a profound gift and every single breath we take is a privilege."

"Without sparing my words, the work we have done with you, Carina, around values and the importance of our routines and reflection, and how we do that, and what that actually looks like day-to-day, has been invaluable to us. We have been complimented by so many people on how successful we have been in managing our expectations and outcomes. I am convinced that it is because our foundation and groundwork included the work we did with you in addressing our values and how to keep them alive in the Polar Night!"

At the beginning of our work together in October 2018, pre-Bamsebu Sunniva was initially reluctant to put time aside for our work. "I simply did not have the time."

After our first call, I asked them to *take time to stop*.

Take the time to look at the very fact that they were busy, and also look at why. They needed to create this time to move forward. I was on them. Held them accountable for showing up for each other. And this was appreciated. They realized they were creating a foundation for something new to emerge.

This work of creating a realistic road map of where you want to go, how, and why, is a foundation for successful teams and self-leadership.

As Hilde and Sunniva agree: "We can all benefit from becoming stronger, better individuals and leaders in our own lives."

Here is where the importance of our work comes in. We explored our behavior patterns and were able to put words to them. Hours of coaching culminated in careful guidance, asking key questions, and surfacing patterns of behavior—both positive and negative.

As human beings we undergo constant change. Reflecting, putting words into thoughts will lead to personal development. The start is the hardest and that is because our brain is lazy. It is so much easier to fall back on familiar paths. This is where the work starts and evolves.

As a coach, I have learned to adapt to the current situation and be flexible, innovative, and use the power in the moment to read the situation and that of my clients.

As coaches, we normally engage face-to-face in a conversation. This was not possible. Not even working via satellite phone offered a solution as there were constant interruptions. I wrote notes instead of speaking in person.

"Carina, the tools you taught us make us realize that now more than ever communication skills and self-assessment around values are critical for our changing world and future leaders. To create a better world, we need to share stories that connect, and we need someone like you to keep checking in and not giving up on us. You believed in us and made us take the time to do this work.

"Thank you for your persistence and your knowledge of what we needed. We were able to go this way, to build a workable framework and successfully meet our goal in Bamsebu."

Hilde and Sunniva have decided to stay until end of September 2020, after a short week in Longyearbyen to resupply, take a shower, and to fill up their supply of coffee.

*Hearts in the Ice: www.heartsintheice.com

References

1. Glaser, J. E. (2014). *Conversational Intelligence: How Great Leaders Build Trust and Get Extraordinary Results.* Brookline, MA: Bibliomotion, Inc.

2. Benchmark Communication®, Inc and Creating WE® Institute

Electronic Resources

Value.Online: https://www.value.se/en/point-of-value

2

Create Your Own "Yellow Brick Road" to Greatness

Elix Cintron

Certified Professional Coach | Speaker | Radio Host
Boston, MA, United States

> "Our goals can only be reached through the vehicle of a plan, in which we must fervently believe, and upon which we must vigorously act. There is no other route to success." ~Pablo Picasso

My unique coaching methodology, G.R.I.P.—an acronym for **Great**ness **R**equires **I**ntention and **P**urpose—is the result of my seventeen years as a professional executive coach. In my experience, individuals who seek coaching aspire to the highest levels of greatness in their business or personal life, and often in both. They are not satisfied with *good* or even *extraordinary*—they want *epic*. G.R.I.P. is a simple tool that can help you navigate the road map necessary to achieve truly epic results.

Of course, I've always known about road maps, but it wasn't until 2017, during my participation in a Conversational Intelligence (C-IQ) training, that I truly understood the impact that a good road map can have as a navigational tool to achieving goals. Now that I am a certified C-IQ coach, I am thrilled to blend Conversational Intelligence concepts into my own work to achieve maximum results for my clients.

C-IQ is about connecting, navigating, and growing alongside others. It provides a framework for building trust—the platform from which our greatest conversations emerge. As we build trust with others, we strengthen our ability to express our own thoughts and feelings, which strengthens our relationships, leading to mutual success.

When we are stuck in a state of distrust, the entire world feels threatening. Threats push us to retreat, making us feel like we need to protect ourselves. According to neuroscience, threats trigger the "reptilian brain," causing an amygdala hijack and heightened cortisol and adrenaline levels. The fear networks in our brains force us to *fight, flee, freeze, or appease.*

If an interaction feels safe and positive, we produce more oxytocin and dopamine. These neurotransmitters create a sense of trust, helping us to relax. Our prefrontal cortex opens up, heightening our empathy, sharpening our judgment, and providing access to our higher decision-making and innovation capabilities. Our heart beats at a steadier rate and we connect with others more deeply.

I want to note that my friend, colleague, and mentor, the late Judith E. Glaser was incredibly influential in integrating Conversational Intelligence to the G.R.I.P. methodology. She was a true pioneer in the field of executive coaching and the author of the book *Conversational Intelligence: How Great Leaders Build Trust and Get Extraordinary Results.* Judith was a great thought partner for me—generously sharing her insights about the importance of a road map to achieving outstanding success.

The letters in G.R.I.P. also stand for the steps we take on our journey: **G**oals, **R**esistance, **I**ntegrity, and **P**lanning. In designing this methodology, I found myself drawn to the image of a yellow brick road. It was only later that I realized my subconscious was trying to tell me something. The yellow brick road, of course, is a powerful symbol in our culture: it is the path that Dorothy Gale must follow in L. Frank Baum's classic children's novel, *The Wonderful Wizard of Oz,* and in the film version that so many of us grew up watching. So, let's have a little fun and reexamine that timeless story through the lens of G.R.I.P. and C-IQ.

Let's follow the yellow brick road...

You're Not in Kansas Anymore

Dorothy's goal is perhaps the simplest of all: to get back home. There was no second-guessing it. She was lost in an unfamiliar land, and her loved ones had no idea where she had gone. The stakes couldn't possibly have been higher.

Every journey must begin with a clear goal. Whether in business or life, knowing what you want is not only important, it is necessary. As a leader, how can you inspire others if you don't have a clear vision of your own? It's like driving around with no destination, just burning gas until the car runs out. I have come across many leaders who "ran out of gas"—not to mention time. Don't let this be you.

Dorothy Gale was committed to her goal. She couldn't imagine going on with her life if she never saw her family again! So, ask yourself: What am I truly, passionately committed to? What is my vision for my future?

> **C-IQ Takeaway:** *Clients often resist goal setting or committing to a specific goal. Why? Mostly out of fear. Fear of failure, fear of looking bad, fear of taking the risk.*

Surrender, Dorothy!

Dorothy felt that her family did not have time for her and therefore did not love her. This assumption led her to run away from home—a rash decision that she came to regret.

How often do we make the same mistake as Dorothy? Something happens in our lives and we immediately interpret it in the most negative way possible, letting our fears fill in the blanks. Before long, we relate to our version of the story as the truth, rather than just the product of our imagination. I've had clients who have quit jobs, or left their spouses, or stopped talking to their loved ones, because they gave power to some made-up story instead of seeking out the facts or directly confronting the people involved. Rather than running away, Dorothy could have asked her family if they loved her. (Although that wouldn't have made for a very interesting story!)

Along the yellow brick road, Dorothy encounters many other roadblocks and obstacles, from flying monkeys to sleep-inducing poppies to the Wicked Witch of the West herself. Often, she has help from others. But life won't always send us a good witch Glinda to lend a helping hand—sometimes we have to find the strength to help ourselves. It takes integrity to soldier through.

> **C-IQ Takeaway:** *When we are in a state of resisting, regretting, or resenting, we are in a state of distrust—a major roadblock for many of us. The result is an amygdala hijack, urging us to fight, flee, freeze, or appease. While in this state, we feel stuck, hopeless, and often addicted to our position—convinced of our "rightness" and everyone else's "wrongness." Developing a conscious awareness of this state is the first step toward moving into a "wait and see" phase, where conditional trust creates an opening to rebuild our integrity.*

A Heart, A Brain, The Nerve

On her journey, Dorothy meets three characters: a self-doubting scarecrow who wishes for a brain, a self-pitying tin man who longs for a heart, and a cowardly lion, who yearns for courage. Inspired by Dorothy's vision, they join her along the yellow brick road.

I've always felt that each of these characters represents something about Dorothy herself. The Dorothy Gale we meet in Kansas is in need of the wisdom of self-confidence (a brain), empathetic passion (a heart), and forthrightness (the nerve). But by the end of her journey, when it comes time to kill the evil witch, Dorothy displays all three, in spades! Her heroic journey—a trip, perhaps, through her own psyche—is really all about building her inner integrity. In this context, integrity has nothing to do with morality. What I'm referring to is *structural* integrity—the wholeness and completeness of one's personal foundation.

C-IQ Takeaway: *Restoring integrity puts you in the "experimenter phase." Here, we engage the prefrontal cortex, the part of our brain that creates trust. When this opens up, we have access to higher decision-making and innovation capabilities, which in turn create an opening for co-creating.*

Head On Down The Road!

Dorothy wouldn't have gotten anywhere if she hadn't taken that first step.

She also wouldn't have gotten anywhere if she hadn't taken all the rest of the steps!

But she had a plan, and she empowered, collaborated, and led her team to follow it. Despite the many obstacles along the way, she remained focused, taking her journey one step at a time. And in the end, she made it home.

Having a clear vision isn't enough. A goal without a written plan is just an illusion. The only way to achieve that vision is by developing a tangible, step-by-step, written plan that takes you from point A to point Z. A plan that only exists in your head is an illusion. How often have you wished for something, only to find that as time went by—days, months, even years—it remained a wish, leaving you feeling unfulfilled, unsatisfied, and unhappy? I would argue that these are significant prices to pay for inaction, and yet so many people remain stuck and hopeless. Don't let this be you! The time is *now* to plan the work and work your plan. Create your own yellow brick road and take that first step into a life of epic proportions. If you, like many others, try to convince yourself that your goal is unrealistic, remember my favorite quote from Will Smith: "Being realistic is the most commonly traveled road to mediocrity." Let me know how that's working out for you!

C-IQ Takeaway: *Dorothy was masterful at co-creating her plan with her three companions. They worked together, helping and rescuing each other. In a sense, they collaborated! Trust was abundant, and the relationship that they built with each other was authentic and pure. Their "WE-centric" way of working was essential to their victory.*

References

Glaser, J. E. (2014). *Conversational Intelligence: How Great Leaders Build Trust and Get Extraordinary Results.* Brookline, MA: Biblio-motion, Inc.

3

Case History: Curiosity, Intentional Listening, and Letting Go

By Grace Moniz
Executive Coaching | Design & Facilitation | Leadership &
Team Development | Inner Change
Manhattan Beach, California, United States

> "Curiosity, intentionally listening, and letting go to let others' ideas flourish, can unlock a team's potential for more effective outcomes." ~Grace Moniz

In an instant, I get a sense of Anita's quiet and sincere leadership presence. Her diminutive stature and quiet nature only momentarily mask her high energy and purposeful gait as she walks through the entrance of the health clinic to greet me. Anita's passion to provide all-access to exceptional patient-centered care resounds in her every step. She is a powerhouse.

Jose, the new human resources director with whom I previously consulted in another health care firm, introduces me to his CEO, Anita.

Meeting the CEO—Building Connection and Trust

Anita, Jose, and I walk along a corridor that houses photos of the development of the first clinic site, from groundbreaking to completion. Anita proudly recounts the organization's history of this multiple-location nonprofit health care organization that provides comprehensive medical, dental, mental health, and pharmaceutical services to the most vulnerable in its community. Since its inception more than fifty years ago, the organization has grown to multiple clinical sites, some of which are innovatively located at elementary schools. The mission is clear: to ensure access to high quality health care to every individual regardless of a person's ability to pay.

With warmth and gratitude Anita shares stories about myriad benefactors who made and continue to sustain the clinics. With curiosity and intentional listening, I absorb all she is saying, asking an occasional question to ensure I understand. In her storytelling I hear what is most important to Anita.

We chat more seriously in a nearby conference room. Our conversation steers toward the CEO's personal history with the organization, her passion for the people served, and what she sees as the clinics' future. I lean forward, curious to learn.

Anita will retire in six years. What she desires most is that the legacy of providing exceptional health care continues for generations to come. She speaks with a sense of urgency, concerned about how to survive the current political climate over health care in the U.S. She wants to know how can she ensure that every member of this organization embodies and sustains her vision of high quality care, regardless of political whim?

As I prod further, Anita begins to articulate her aspirations for this institution, laying out what needs to change for the clinics to succeed. She paints from her mind a detailed picture of the future organization. How does she embed her vision to create a legacy that transcends generations…a culture of excellent family care that passes from one generation to the next? What can she do, she asks, to ensure all levels of the company see and are part of this vision?

Confident her vision is in alignment with her core executive leadership team, Anita invites two of its members, the chief medical officer (CMO) and chief operating officer (COO), to join us. I learn as much as possible about these two leaders who have the trust of the CEO. Mentally, I note areas of similarities and differences as their answers only lead to further questions. Something begins to open up—a need beyond just sharing the CEO's vision.

What begins as an opportunity to meet and develop trust with the CEO unexpectedly emerges into a decision to design and deliver a one-day leadership retreat. I agree to meet with the entire core executive team and facilitate a discovery session to draw out everyone's concerns and needs for the organization, and to lay a fruitful foundation for a full-day leadership engagement.

Meeting the Core Executive Team—Discovery

As I prepare to engage senior leaders in a discovery session, I set my intentions to be curious and draw out multiple perspectives. I set intentions to build trust and rapport, and to listen to discover, assure understanding, and verify meaning. Setting intentions prepares and grounds me. I am not the expert in health care or in what solutions would resolve their greatest concerns. I am here to learn. I am here to draw out, through my questions, *their* ideas.

For two hours, leaders share their concerns and challenges within their respective areas of responsibility. I listen, ask questions, and listen more. They express what is most important to address in the leadership retreat. My fingers fly across the keyboard as I capture as many of the leaders' own words and phrases as possible. Multiple pages of notes describe needs throughout the organization. The gamut runs from decision-making, accountability, and instilling a new model of patient care to breaking down silos and improving communications across sites. In my mind, common themes fuse into organized images.

The team prioritizes the desired outcomes for the leadership retreat. Candor, frankness, and an ability to calmly and respectfully express a divergence of ideas flow through the session with ease. By the members' interactions and transparency, it is clear this team has developed trust with one another under Anita's leadership.

Conceptual Development—Envision

Anita's vision to create a "legacy of excellence that transcends generations" becomes the cornerstone of my thought as I consider elements for the retreat. I reflect on other stated objectives: a) align and move the company forward, b) build cooperative cross-functional entities, and c) enable each person to see him/herself as part of the whole. To achieve this, we will need to create a common understanding, language, and image about Anita's vision that can cascade through every level of the organization. "How" is the next question to be answered.

Beginning with a goal to ensure that each exercise has a defined purpose aligned to an objective, I read and reread notes from the discovery session. I ponder abounding engagement solutions— reflective experiences, games, drawings, paired and group dialogue. I begin to envision the "how."

Absorbing the data, I imagine myself a participant and ask myself this key question, "What is the experience that will give me the desired outcome?" If the objective is to help a team learn new ways to communicate more effectively, developing listening skills is key. What experiences can I provide so participants feel the positive neurochemical impact of deep mutual listening and being heard? Once someone experiences the encouraging effects of a new behavior, she/he is more inclined to repeat it.

For weeks I contemplate the day unfolding. Imagery empowers the mind, and I envision the day in vivid details. When I make the time to meditate, reread notes, and picture myself as a participant I am able to organize and visualize experiences that meet deliverables.

Designing the experiences for the retreat is done. Each element aligns to a specific objective and I now turn my attention to the venue. Aware of the importance of the physical environment, I set parameters for a site with round tables, windows that access the outdoors, and pleasant colors that contribute to a warm ambiance.

Co-Creation with Executive Leadership Team—Letting Go

Two months ahead of the retreat I meet with the executive leadership team to review the design of the day's event. "Giving a gift" reverberates in my mind like a mantra as I offer what I have designed for the day as a gift to them. This is their retreat; I am only a vessel that translates their vision into experiences.

Letting go, I invite the leaders to join me as the retreat's co-creators, to imagine, explore, innovate, and design together the experiences of the day. It is a risk I take, to involve the leaders. In the past I have been entrusted "as the consultant" to come up with a solution and deliver it. This time, I want to experiment with co-creation. What would be different if I invite the leaders' participation? Step-by-step I talk about each activity and share its purpose, intended outcome, and how the experience aligns with an objective for the day. I let go of any attachment to what I created and wait for their response. To my relief, heads nod in approval.

Palpable energy and excitement flows as leaders converse with one another. I quietly fade into the background and watch. Ideas begin to gently fine-tune the retreat's activities. Jose adds a text-enabled evaluation feature; senior members want the CEO to introduce the event and share her vision as descriptively as possible. Her passion and sense of urgency are quite convincing! With a finalized design, I shift the conversation to how to market the retreat to the other forty-plus leaders.

Breaking down positional, hierarchical, and geographic silos (doctors versus all other positions, as an example) is a primary outcome for the leadership retreat. Yet I notice the leaders discuss two avenues of marketing and communications: one for providers (doctors and dentists) and one for everyone else! Organizations sometimes lack awareness of how their behaviors work against their stated values and intentions; they unwittingly behave in ways that sustain a culture they want to change. How do I gently raise awareness of this situation?

Calming the butterflies in my stomach I ask to speak. "May I share what I am observing?" Heads nod with permission. "What is one of the objectives for the retreat?" I ask and wait in silence. Awareness begins to set in. Laughing, they recognize their misdirection and decide to create one message for all. Asking, "What is that message?" stirs a lot of discussion.

The team talks about making the retreat mandatory, and how important it is for every leader to be present. When the conversation shifts to consequences of not being there, my heart drops. I can feel the negative, contracting energy. I ask permission to speak and pause. "Imagine a different scenario, a different possibility," I offer. "What if the retreat is voluntary? Imagine receiving an invitation to an exceptional leadership retreat, an event you don't want to miss?" (Pause.)

Energy slowly begins to shift to the positive. Nodding heads affirm the new direction for marketing the event. Creative bursts of ideas begin to flow anew, as people begin planning other details of the event.

The CMO (chief medical officer) excitedly recalls other events where "we walked into the room and took off our name badges and titles." He vividly describes the positive learning climate created when turning over nametags fostered mutual respect. We agree— without titles, judgment dissipates and openness to ideas expands.

To emphasize that every person has value, regardless of position or title, the leaders decide to place multiple leadership levels at each table and at least one representative from each clinic location. Sharing at a table comprised of people from multiple locations facilitates the development of cross-functional, cross-locational communication and interaction. Yes, I think, this setup will serve to break down silos.

The dam of ideas among these capable leaders breaks open and more decisions are rapidly made about the retreat:

- Clinics will be closed on the day of the retreat signifying the retreat's importance to the organization.
- Attendance at the retreat is voluntary.
- Leaders positively position the event as one not to be missed and promote with one marketing communication for all fifty-five leaders.
- Anita, a gifted writer, offers to pen the marketing communications. Team members volunteer to review and edit the communications.
- Every executive commits to personally inviting leaders in their respective departments.
- Jose commits the Human Resources team to support behind-the-scenes efforts.

For the first time in this organization's history, all fifty-five leaders voluntarily attend the all-day event.

ExperiMentor Mindset—Day of Retreat

> "Playfully exploring new experiences with an "ExperiMentor" mindset gives us permission to unleash our creativity—often with the freedom of a child. Not only do we have fun when creativity sparks, when done collectively with others a positive emotional contagion fills the room, a concept I learned from Judith."
>
> ~Grace Moniz

To begin the morning, I invite people to participate, explore, and have fun. We meditate, envision, draw, and converse. We laugh and share and learn together. I walk around and listen. A kind and calm cadence enhances their conversations at tables throughout the session and during breaks. Every person participates; every person shares his/her ideas without fear or judgment. By the end of the day, fifty-five leaders share a common understanding of what it means to live "a legacy of excellence that transcends generations," in words, images, and committed actions.

A few months following the retreat Jose provides an update as to what has transpired in the organization. Daily conversations have changed. People, aware of the assumptions they make, seek to understand and create shared meaning by "Double-Clicking," a term coined by Judith E. Glaser. As Judith explained, when we Double-click on a word in a document, a dictionary, thesaurus, and synonyms pop up as options to learn more about a particular word's meaning. "May I Double-click on that?" is often heard. They assume positive intentions now. One table of participants across multiple sites who developed close ties at the event continues to meet. A renewed energy refreshes the organization.

Summary—Reflection

Most helpful to initiating this successful engagement were listening and curiosity. Setting the intention to listen, truly listen with multiple senses, steadied my focus on what the other person was communicating. Small micro-expressions across the face, a light movement in the body, and an elevated tone in one's voice each provided a clue to a deeper message and of course, more questions. People felt heard. Listening with intention yielded rich connections.

Insatiable curiosity to learn about leaders and their concerns and aspirations led to the thorough understanding necessary to create the initial design of the customized retreat. Not staying with the first given response, curiosity prompted more questions and the answers were essential to the effective outcome. A curious mindset drew out and expanded possibilities for everyone, as curiosity became part of the energy of the retreat, too. Modeling exploring and asking open-ended questions helped people behave and communicate in new ways.

Coupled with listening and insatiable curiosity, drawing out the expertise of the leaders themselves proved invaluable in this engagement. Letting go of what I had developed for the day opened the door for mutual exploration among the executive leadership team. Their participation in codesigning the final experiences generated a lot of excitement and contagious enthusiasm that carried through to all fifty-five leaders prior to and during the retreat. This co-creation alone significantly contributed to the retreat's success.

Curiosity, intentionally listening, and letting go to let others' ideas flourish, can unlock a team's potential for more effective outcomes.

4

Moving from "Stuck" to Lasting Change

By Charlotte Weston-Horsmann
Executive Coach|Intercultural Communication Specialist|
Team Coaching|Leadership Development
Bernried, Germany

> "The real voyage of discovery consists not in seeking new landscapes but in having new eyes." ~ Marcel Proust

Why is it that despite our best efforts to tap into our most compelling aspirations, we find it so difficult to commit to the changes that would enable us to move forward? What does it take for us to rewrite old narratives that no longer serve us and step up to our best possible selves and our truly meaningful aspirations?

The ability to create and sustain lasting change remains maddingly elusive. Given that this is so potent—how can we begin to surface the behavioral patterns that we are largely unaware of and that keep us stuck? These patterns served our distant ancestors to protect us from real, rather than perceived, threats. In our collective atavistic memory, we still perceive the proverbial saber-toothed tiger lurking somewhere ready to destroy us.

Perceived life-threatening situations have evolved into ego— protecting behavior, much of which can be observed in our interactions and the conversations we have with each other. There are assumptions around what threatens or keeps us safe, and we have built our mindsets around this. We seek out psychological safety in "comfort bubbles" and as members of a "tribe," where our way of being feels natural to us, where we are accepted and socially validated. This certainly comes as no surprise.

Our neurological circuitry is programmed for homeostasis to keep us balanced, healthy, and thriving. But the balance is also precarious. What if one day we begin feeling the edginess, frustration or even health issue calling to us that something within us is wanting—no, craving to emerge? Or maybe we've had an epiphany of sorts that lifted the lid off the bell jar we'd been living under. Or maybe a new awareness drawing larger circles, urging us to overcome the stuckness and step up to exploring new "lifescapes" of possibility, of more meaningful connectedness in our relationships and work.

Change manifests outside in the external world and is visible. Transformation, on the other hand, happens internally. This sheds some light on why we make ourselves immune to change. Change required or imposed on us from an external source that questions or even threatens our beliefs and basic assumptions about ourselves will meet with resistance. Our immune system kicks in to protect the way we are or do things. The desire and motivation develop intrinsically as the danger-sensing immune system Down-Regulates. Over time, as the system embeds new insights, perspectives, and learning, transformation and sustainable change emerges.

Making the Invisible Visible: Looking Beneath the Surface

I'd like to take you, the reader, on an exploratory journey to a place where personal transformation lives. It takes guts and grit to point the spotlight at what keeps us from stepping into our own light.

There is this saying, "When the student is ready, the teacher will appear." And so it must have been when I heard about Conversational Intelligence, the certification program launched by the late Judith E. Glaser of Benchmark Communication, Inc. I signed up and embarked on a life-changing learning journey. Module by module in peer learning groups, participants gained an in-depth view of how core beliefs, basic assumptions about ourselves and the world around get stuck in protective behavior modes that influence interactions. The conversations we have, the deep listening we do, and the language we use find the "the crack in the wall" through which we have the opportunity to connect on a fundamental level and build the trust it takes to create meaningful relationships.

Based on sound neuroscientific research, Ms. Glaser walked participants through the process of how the brain rewires to shift into thinking and acting in ways that "convey our inner thoughts and feelings to one another that strengthen relationships and success"[1] With every step, she "walked her talk", expressing her own vulnerability, leaning into the learning journey, and showing how to embody the language that shifts energy toward inclusion and co-creation in relationships.

I began taking a closer look at the quality of language I use and the responses I was getting: What are the biases popping up? What is triggering me? Is my language accusatory, defensive or belittling? Instead of ruminating about where I had missed the mark, I asked myself: *How do I want people to feel as a result of engaging with me in a conversation? Safe and valued? Truly listened to and curious about how they think and feel?* Yes, all of those. And how do I hold and sustain the space where conversations of this nature can unfold? How do I Down-Regulate toxic moments by shifting into behavior and language that activates the bonding hormone, oxytocin, that signals safety and nurtures trust?

I began identifying communication patterns I had developed that didn't "hit the mark." Over the years in my relationships and coaching work, it has become increasingly important to me to understand the drivers behind my own behavior and actions. Once I learned to monitor my thinking, shift behavior, and use language that connects rather than overpowers or threatens, I experienced a game-changing insight: every conversation holds the promise of turning into an authentic, co-creative, and meaningful experience. But first, dare to face the gremlins!

Why "Immunity" to Change?

The learning was intriguing. I was inspired to learn more about surfacing unconscious behavior that keeps us stuck in repetitive patterns that don't serve.

My next journey led me to an online course based on the book, *Immunity to Change*[1], by authors Robert Kegan and Lisa Lahey. They cite a study conducted in 2009 that showed how our habits "have us" and cause us to resist change even under extreme circumstances. The report cites that when doctors tell heart patients they will die if they don't change their habits, only one in seven will be able to follow through successfully. Even under such life-threatening circumstances patients, while truly desiring and motivated to change, are unable to sustain the kind of behavior that could save their life. What does that say for the rest of us in less than life-threatening situations? What if stepping out of our comfort bubbles constitutes something similar, such as an identity-threatening situation?

We tend to "create a natural and powerful immunity to change."[2] There is good reason for the immunity described here. The composite of our heritage, e.g. upbringing, cultural heritage, life experiences, and challenges that we have learned to deal with to the best of our ability have evolved into an integral part of our belief systems. Our belief systems embody our values and filter the way we perceive our environment and interactions. They ensure basic human needs of safety and a sense of belonging, feed assumptions, and act like an anxiety-management system.

Seen from this perspective, and like the word itself suggests, immunity to change has a protective function. We create competing (or hidden) commitments that serve to validate our assumptions. But the intrinsic belief system that underlies the way we think and navigate in the world doesn't always serve our best interests nor those of others.

Overcoming our own immunity to change requires us to challenge our limiting beliefs and habitual thought patterns that have a hold over us. Why do we keep repeating well-worn behavioral patterns intended to keep us "safe"? Stepping away from our habitual mindset and the corresponding identity we've espoused takes courage.

The title "Immunity to Change" (ITC) first caught my attention in a session given by Lisa Lahey at the WBECS Community of Coaches Summit. Like many others, I've experienced this stuck feeling at regular intervals. Not being able to identify its source, I was prone to feeling frustrated, angry, and shamed but still able to muddle through somehow. I was intrigued. "Wow, what if I had clarity around all the things I do that keep me stuck in areas of my life that are really important to me?" This was immediately followed by "I'd be living a more authentic version of myself, knowing what I needed to be the best possible me!" *Wow!*

The Journey: First Steps

Equipped with Robert Kegan and Lisa Lahey's book and the help of a certified ITC colleague and coach, I ventured forth. My first task was to identify my Main Improvement Goal. Contrary to recommendations, I decided to go all out instead of taking the recommended small steps. After some soul-searching, I came up with, "I want to live my signature self." The question that had to follow was…"and what does that look like?" It was like slowly drawing open a curtain and watching a scenario take shape. I noticed my breathing slowing down and becoming deeper and my shoulders straightening. I felt physically strong and emotionally composed as in my mind's eye I stepped up to the podium in front of a group of expectant faces. I was confident, "I am okay, and this is going to be okay, I am safe in who I am and what I have to share."

Still savoring this feeling of safety and composure, the next question brought me back to the moment, "What are you doing or not doing that inhibits your improvement goal?" I immediately perceived the difference between the first and second scenarios. I pondered the second question and slowly faced my first demon. "I tell myself I'm not good enough and that I don't belong. People won't like me. I can't trust people. They will judge me negatively." This stuff didn't feel so good.

Next, came questions about "competing commitments." In other words, I am committed to protecting myself; hence always on the lookout for signs that will confirm assumptions about not being good enough. I began to understand the idea about being held captive by: 1) assumptions we hold about ourselves and the world, and 2) by measures we take to confirm those assumptions. The outward behavior manifested in defensiveness and aloofness, suspicion that something potentially psychologically painful could occur at any moment.

> "The concept of hijacking one's own best intentions becomes painfully clear."
> ~Charlotte Weston-Horsmann

I began to understand that we are deeply committed to upholding assumptions about ourselves and the world around us. Even while aspiring to change, we are often unaware of competing commitments that work against improvement goals and hold us captive. And here, like with an autoimmune reaction that rejects something the body actually needs, the hidden commitments hijack best intentions to keep us "safe" or aligned with our assumptions.

Together with my certified ITC coach, we walked through the process of uncovering Blind Spots and descending into an underworld of competing commitments. Remember, competing commitments are those little devils that "protect" from a change that might shake up your world view (and identity!).

Looking Back to Look Forward: Where the Big Assumptions Originated

Strangely enough, long dormant memories of a key event from early childhood kept sliding into focus. There may be no scientific explanation for this, but it seemed to me as if there was a direct line of connection.

The first years of my life were spent in Monterey, California. What I remember of that time was tagging along with my older brothers in their cast-off jeans and T-shirts to explore the nearby pine forests and sand dunes. My older brother, Bill, always wore his signature Davy Crockett cap with the attached racoon tail trailing down his back. The days seemed endless. My brother ferreted out different weird-looking reptiles and spiders to add to his collection in his "pioneer room." I was fascinated. We returned home tired and dirty, with me walking between my brothers, each hand held tightly in one of theirs.

Just before my fifth birthday we packed up and moved to a small town in Bavaria close to the Austrian border. We moved in with my German grandmother who had escaped the Allied bombing of Berlin. We were six people in very close quarters, and I remember this time as a deeply felt sense of belonging, nestled safely in a warm family cocoon. But we were independent kids— accustomed to exploring our surroundings, which we did with great gusto.

One experience shortly after our arrival may have impacted the trajectory of my life in a significant way. The kids in our neighborhood played on the dirt streets and explored the forbidden haunts around the local sawmill just down the road. Naturally, I was curious and ventured out into this new territory. I was not a fearful child—curiosity always got the better of me—which was the case when I saw a group of kids about my own age down the way. I approached them eagerly, not realizing that they may be different in some way from the playmates I knew back home. It also didn't occur to me at the moment that they spoke another language although I knew quite well from my father that people spoke German in Germany. That was far from my mind as I happily approached the group and introduced myself, "Hi, my name is Jacky!"

They looked at me and my beat-up hand-me-down jeans as if I were something from outer space. They backed away and began talking among themselves, looking at…no staring at me from top to bottom. Then one of the boys in worn lderhosen pointed at me, and the group began laughing. I was mortified. Something was wrong…I was wrong! What was happening? When harsh words mingled with laughter struck me, something shifted…I remember crying out in a trembling voice, "Sticks and stones will break my bones, but words will never hurt me." How wrong I was! The initial curiosity turned to fear as a feeling I didn't understand took hold of my senses. I had never experienced rejection or humiliation before. In my confusion I turned and ran with the laughter still ringing in my ears.

Slowly, the fog began to clear, and I could see these stories from an adult perspective and understand what they stood for: just old narratives and relics of past experiences. I can let them go. They no longer serve me.

Diagnosing the Immunity to Change®: Cracking the Code

When speaking up to voice an opinion or an idea, I very often feel a pull toward a voice in the back of my mind telling me, "You're no good; you're not okay." Having nurtured the assumptions created during life's journey, these little devils had apparently found a comfortable host. From here they could keep a foot on the brake— always "protecting" from some unconsciously perceived danger and destabilizing natural and healthy intent. A tug-of-war emerged between feeling the "you're not okay" voice and the vibrant pull toward stepping out and being heard.

The challenge is to become aware of this tug-of-war, take a good hard look, and choose differently. It will take stepping away and understanding that unwarranted fear is just a smoke screen. It will take a first test, then another until the smoke clears and stepping into what feels like true self becomes natural.

The first test came soon enough. I was asked to speak in front of a large group of "experts" on a topic I'm passionate about. This is a situation I have more or less successfully avoided, keeping me under the radar in terms of my professional aspirations. I felt the little devils pulling at the gut strings and was familiar with that story. But that narrative was now behind me, on the other side of the smoke screen! There was no falling back, only moving forward. It was truly a release and I began preparing with full vigor.

When the time came for my presentation and although I was aware of the old story, it no longer "had" me. I was able to stand in front of the audience and be fully present. I spoke and moved with intent and clarity. I was able to "read the air" and inspire curiosity in the room. The follow-up Q&A session reinforced this engagement and most important for me, the feeling that I was indeed an accepted and respected member of the tribe. This initial peak experience has since become my anchor when stepping up to speak. I love what I do. I no longer judge myself. And…guess what? I'm okay! I'm in my signature presence.

Resources

[1] Judith E. Glaser, *Conversational Intelligence: How Great Leaders Build Trust and Get Extraordinary Results*, Bibliomotion, Inc., Bookline, MA 02445, 2014

[2] R. Kegan and L. Lahey, *Immunity to Change,* inside book cover, Harvard Business Press, Boston Massachusetts, 2009

[3] Caroline Miller provides a short summary of the mapping steps including an example on her website: https://www.carolinemiller.com/do-you-have-immunity-to-change/.

[4] R. Kegan and L. Lahey, *How the Way We Talk Can Change the Way We Work*, p. 78, San Francisco: Jossey-Bass, 2001

Further Reading: R. Kegan and L. Lahey, *The Real Reason People Won't Change*, Harvard Business Review, November 2001

5

Case Study: Navigating Personal Transformation

By Jane Owen
Women's Leadership & Transitions Coach
London, UK

> "I held a limiting belief that I never have enough time. This belief constrained me, created stress, and impacted my wellbeing." Jane Owen

An inbox of hundreds of new messages greets me as I arrive at my office. Messages are replicated in three different accounts, instant messaging platforms, WhatsApp groups, text messages, and voicemails. Add to this bombardment of "demands" to my attention are Facebook, Slack workspaces, Twitter feeds, and LinkedIn blogs.

The pressure and distractions are endless. I am left unfocused and unproductive, paralysed to take action. I feel socially isolated with feelings of irritability and overwhelm, frequent terms used to describe the consequences of twenty-first century living.

How do I break out of this endless message overload cycle and increase my productivity and wellbeing for my own benefit and those around me?

Joining the Conversational Intelligence (C-IQ) certification programme with Judith E. Glaser in 2017 provided the answer. Over the past two years I have been on a journey to experiment and embody C-IQ to create lasting change.

During the second module of the certification programme Judith introduced the concept of road maps, a series of organised steps in a process to simplify the complex. Road maps are recognised universally. According to neuroscience our brains respond well to road maps because they stimulate connections between our memory and our logical and creative neurons. In other words, establishing a connection between our neocortex and prefrontal cortex.

The key point here is that by creating a road map for yourself, you are already creating a different space from which you can take a new view or perspective. I encourage you to notice where you use road maps. My focus now is on the road map PACE, learnt during C-IQ certification.

What is PACE?

P	Physical Space
A	Aspirational Space
C	Co-Creative Space
E	Emotional Space

PACE represents four individual dimensions: Physical, Aspirational, Co-Creative, and Emotional. Each dimension when given attention and focus expands the inner and outer space in our minds. This in turn expands our capability.

1. PACE: Physical
What is Physical Space?

Physical space is the unlimited expanse of our universe in which all material objects are located. To make sense of this I consider my body as a physical space and assess, for example, what is going on inside my brain, my heart, and my gut. My outer space is the environment in which I operate. Both of these spaces are conducive to me being my best self. In taking this perspective I have been able to make small adjustments to open up my physical space to improve my behaviour just as open space improves children's behaviour[1].

I experimented with the physical aspect of space. For example, when I had conversations at home I experimented with where I sat in relation to others and assessed the impact physical space had on conversational effectiveness. Our table is rectangular and when I sat tucked behind a kitchen unit partially hidden from others I observed I would often be ignored or not included in a conversation. When I sat at the other end of the table I could be seen easily and integrated into the conversation. Other experiments have included going to the person whose attention I need rather than shouting up the stairs; and taking individuals outside the home or workspace to have difficult and/or important conversations.

How Physical Space Affected a Client

The client presented with stress, bordering on depression. The client was involved in delivering a long-term project for the organisation they worked for. During this time the client went from enjoyment of their role to feeling incredibly trapped and frustrated. What shifted in their physical environment to create these feelings?

There had been an organisational restructure and the introduction of hot desking designed to support flexible working. Hot desking created a competitive environment and increased stress and frustration. There were never enough desks to go round and teams working on the same projects rarely got to sit together. In addition, everyone at a desk had their head down and/or headphones on and wished not to be interrupted. Combined, these physical changes reduced people's interaction to almost zero.

This change in physical space led to a lack of conversation and led to the client experiencing feelings of isolation. Through our coaching we discussed how to experiment and change the physical environment. The client decided to sit at a round table by a door for the day rather than at a hot desk. The client discovered in that location people would stop and speak, engaging in a few minutes of casual conversation._These small interactions elevated the mood of the client.

Simultaneously when the client worked from home they experimented with the physical space. Normally when this client worked at home, they sat at a desk associated with their work for this particular organization. When they sat at this desk for this organization, they stayed in the frustration they experienced from the monotony of the work they were doing and their isolation. This prevented the client from taking the necessary actions to transform their career. One day the client chose to work in the lounge, away from their desk. The new physical space moved them into a new emotionally positive space, so they were then able to work more productively on their aspirations and future career.

This small experiment of focusing on the physical external space triggered a shift in my client's mind-set or mind space. The client found the courage to take control to make new connections and re-establish old ones, and in the process secured a new, broader role in the same organisation moving from a contractor to a permanent staff member in the process.

Questions to Ask Yourself

- Consider your physical space. Is it conducive to what you want?
- How can you alter your physical space to get different results?

2. PACE- Aspirational
What is Aspirational Space?

In the PACE road map A refers to aspiration, which is the desire or ambition to achieve something. Aspirations require us to dream, which our brains can do consciously or unconsciously. Aspirational space gives us access not only to the thoughts in our head but also to what we are feeling in our heart and gut. Access to these three dimensions offers a bigger space for us to uncover possibilities beyond the here and now to create positive change.

Case Study

The Positive Aspects of the Aspirational Space

The client was uncomfortable with carrying out performance reviews and, particularly, shifting the conversation into a career development discussion in the same meeting.

The client was comfortable talking about setting expectations. Expectations are defined as the belief that something will happen, or a problem will be solved. Expectations access only our thoughts and are external to us.

Talking about expectations first proved useful in the performance discussions but often faltered in getting any discussion going about career development and kept them very narrowly focused on the next area for development or the next role.

The client experimented and focused first on aspirations; the client shared the definition of an aspiration and then shared some of their own aspirations for the conversation. This primed the space for asking the team member what their aspirations were. This one word *aspiration* shifted the conversation and both parties shared more honestly and thought more strategically. As a consequence, the client began to understand whether their team member's aspirations were to stay or leave the organisation and the client was then able to produce a more authentic succession plan.

Questions to Ask Yourself

- What are your aspirations for your career?
- What are your one hundred aspirations for life?
- How does this compare to your expectations?

3. PACE Co-Creation
What is Co-Creational Space?

The *C* in PACE stands for co-creation and refers to the space available for new possibilities to emerge in conversation with ourselves and others when the conditions are conducive.

What are the Conditions for a Co-creative Space?

Trust is a prerequisite to expand the co-creative space available for possibilities to emerge. If we examine what we mean by TRUST, Judith E. Glaser would refer to another road map and say it consists of the following five elements:

1. *Transparency,* the quality of being genuine and authentic.

2. *Relationship,* focused on connecting with another individual.

3. To connect one has to seek to *Understand* the other rather than to judge.

4. *Sharing* successes of your positive results.

5. *Truth Telling,* stating what one really thinks and feels, which can sometimes be difficult to do and difficult to hear. This can be true of our relationship with oneself, our "inner space," as well as the relationship with others, the "outer space." [3].

Case History

How I Created Co-creational Space

Early in the Conversation Intelligence programme I was very keen to experiment and share with my husband the Conversational Dashboard™ model I had learned.

It is a model for identifying levels of trust between individuals, teams, and even organisations. It enables individuals to identify where they are in relation to any particular issue, problem, or challenge and ask themselves what it will take to shift into a more trusting space.

The dashboard model also identifies different levels of communication associated with the different levels of trust. At its

First Level	Instruction
Second Level	Influencing Power-Over Someone
Third Level	Sharing and Discovering Power-With Someone

most simple form, a Level I Conversation requires little trust, a Level II Conversation requires conditional trust, and a Level III Conversation requires complete trust.

I was very excited to share the three conversational levels with my husband and ask him where he was on the Conversational Dashboard™ in relation to the concept of the dashboard. At that moment his response was "What do you want me to say?" I felt deflated and realised that I was in Level II, trying to persuade him rather than being in Level III Conversation open to influence and connecting with him. At that point I pushed the model to the side and said, "Your response really frustrated me." He pointed out that I was pushing something onto him.

This was followed by a discussion about our different approaches to problem solving. When I talk about an issue or a problem, I just need to talk about it and I don't need another person to solve it for me. His approach is that he simply wants to help and provide a solution or what's the point of talking about it if you don't need help?

We then moved on to solving a problem about how to deal with issues arising with our children. From a Level III Conversation—showing vulnerability, being open to influence, and listening to connect: we co-created a text code (IDWI-I deal with it, YDWI-you deal with it, WDWI-we deal with it) that I could use when describing a situation via text that indicted the action being taken so that he understood whether I required any action from him. It has been particularly useful in avoiding frustration when managing issues with our children.

Questions to Ask Yourself

- What do you do to open up the conversational spaces?
- What do you want to co-create?
- Who with?
- How can you do this?

4. PACE Emotional

The *E* in PACE stands for emotional space and refers to feelings that can take up space just as time and energy do. Have you ever noticed that emotions can crowd a room? If someone is exceptionally emotional their emotion can take over and other people tone their emotions down.

There are different aspects to emotional space. The general principle is that we develop more emotional control as we grow up. This can get interpreted as the need to suppress our emotions or that there is something wrong with emotion, particularly those that cause pain or other perceived negative feelings. However, holding on to emotions that belong to a past can restrict our emotional space causing us to get triggered in current situations. So, what can increase our emotional space, and enable us to be in our prefrontal cortex?

I think it starts with creating a safe space for both ourselves and for others. Once again that starts with trust. When we feel safe to express our feelings in the presence of others neuroscientifically there is positive emotional contagion. When this exists, we create mirror neurons in one another's brains sometimes referred to as flow state (Mihaly Csikszentmihayi flow theory.) Even heartbeats have been shown to be in rhythm [4].

Creating More Space by Processing Emotion

Expanding the space for personal transition often requires us to challenge beliefs that might be holding us back.

I was fortunate enough to work with some outstanding colleagues that demonstrated a great example of holding a supportive safe space for me to expand my emotional space. In this safe space I talked about an event from my childhood that I had not had the capacity to process at the time. I was able to release the emotion and let the associated beliefs go. By letting go of the emotion, I created space for a new set of beliefs.

Case Study

Holding the emotional space for a client requires you to stay in Level III Conversation, listening to connect, asking questions for which you have no answers, and sustaining conversation agility by refocusing, redirecting, or reframing.

In this particular instance my client had been asked to pay to attend a conference they were leading due to the mismanagement of finances by the member organisation for which the conference was being run. My client was feeling enormous resentment and it was dominating their whole being. They were talking without breathing, contorted physically, truly uncomfortable with the situation they found themselves in.

My client was conflicted. On the one hand they were finding this request to pay grossly unfair and wanted to withdraw from the organisation of the event. On the other hand, in their mind it was not that simple.

First, my client needed to support an individual who would otherwise be left to manage the conference on their own without the skills. Second, for the first time my client had designed a conference they believed would be impactful for the organisation's members and would result in lasting change for its members.

Listening to connect and providing a reframe to seeing the conference design as a case study for designing future events opened up the possibility that my client could sell the design to other organisations. Looking at the situation through this new lens enabled my client to see this event as an investment of time and money and cut out the noise created by the dysfunctional organisation for which she was designing the conference.

Cutting out the noise resonated with my client. In that moment, my client closed the door on the dysfunctional organisation and immediately felt more confident, calmer, and peaceful. The resentment was gone! By creating the space for emotions to be expressed we co-created a broader perspective and a healthier way of being.

Questions to Ask Yourself (to Expand Emotional Space)

- What can you do to observe your emotional state?
- What patterns are there?
- What triggers an emotional state?
- How are you feeling right now?

Applying PACE

While working with a client returning to work in a large investment bank after a break of twelve years, we agreed as an experiment to use the PACE road map. This was possible because we had already created high levels of trust in prior work together. We decided to use PACE as a way to review and hold us to account through our sessions. This led to further experiments and co-creations with space.

One of our aspirations for the coaching contract was to have fun and "play with the four different spaces of PACE." This included using physical objects to represent situations and people. We used pictures instead of words to capture our learning. We played with the physical space in which we did our work, walking and sitting in different spaces. In carrying out these experiments we discovered an increased co-creative space. My client then carried out these experiments in her organisation. The experiments increased the quality of relationships, which in turn increased the quality of output. My client was rewarded with a promotion. The PACE road map proved a valuable road map in her transformation.

Taking It Further...

Start by setting your own PACE and in turn think about a team and perhaps your organisation.

I held a limiting belief that I never have enough time. This belief constrained me, created stress, and impacted my wellbeing. I now have a new, very powerful belief that I create space, all sorts of space. For me this new belief is expansive, empowering, and liberating. I am no longer in overwhelm; I start my day in a different space with a walk in the park. Although a day is still twenty-four hours, I have twenty-four hours of space. With this new wisdom, I achieve even more.

References

1. K.Ball J.Salmon Health & Space (2006).
2. *Conversational Intelligence: How Great Leaders build Trust and get Extraordinary Results*, Judith E. Glaser
3. Daniel A. Bochner PH.D.www.drbochner.com
4. The Science of HeartMath www.heartmath.com

6

Transparency as a Catalyst for a Healthy and Sustainable Culture

By Ute Franzen-Waschke
Coaching Across Hierarchies| Facilitation| Workshop
& Program Design
Holle, Germany

> "Before you speak, ask yourself:
> Is it kind, is it necessary, does it improve upon
> the silence?"
> ~Shirdi Sai Baba

Consider the word *transparency* and the following questions:

How much transparency can *you*—as an employee of an organization—handle?

How much as an organization can you and should you trust your employees when sharing information?

How transparent can organizations be with their employees?

These questions come up again and again both in private conversations as well as in coaching sessions with individuals and teams/groups. So, my guess is that *transparency* seems to be a controversially discussed topic.

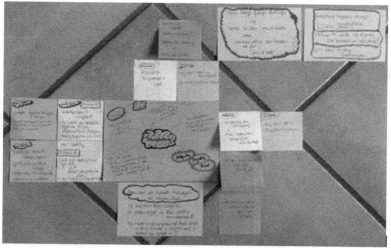

This sticky note collection of what I had heard from clients around the topic of transparency illustrates the many facets transparency seems to have in the corporate world.

Important learning when looking at the collection and its diversity: start conversations on transparency— as we in C-IQ (Conversational Intelligence) would say— by Double-Clicking on what "being transparent in the workplace" means to those involved in the conversation. As often there are so many perspectives on and different contexts in which the term transparency is used, consequently it can also lead to different approaches and serve different needs.

Statements I have heard about the meaning of transparency can be categorized as follows:

Pro-transparency Comments:

"I can tell you everything."

"I say everything I know."

"Transparency is all about giving feedback." (Another note to myself: Is it really!? What is the connection between transparency and feedback? What is the purpose of each? Definitely something to be explored in future conversations with my clients and worth another thought-provoking article.)

Con-transparency Comments:

"It's too much...if they knew everything, they would worry too much and not work/engage enough."

"Parents also do not tell their children everything."

"It's simply too dangerous and risky. News will be shared even though it is flagged as confidential, therefore, we cannot be transparent all the time."

Some of the above statements would be excellent conversation topics for round table discussions, mini Town Hall meetings or informal fireside chats, where organizations could engage people across hierarchies: executives, middle managers, team members, everyone from the highest ranks to the lowest, the more mixed the groups the better, and the smaller the better.

Sending vs. Receiving Mode

These statements are so rich and so valuable. If explored and unpacked in smaller circles rather than larger circles (or not at all), real conversations and exchanges can take place and not just monologues where views and expectations are dumped by those that are in "sending mode" on those that are in "receiving mode." This small difference in having a real conversation could have a huge impact on improving the situation not only around transparency but also on how things are done in the organization.

Intention and Impact

Another observation is that intention and impact when being transparent can differ considerably. Let's take a look at the con-transparency statements.

You could say: Yes, management is truly concerned about the well-being of their staff.

And you could say: management is afraid that engagement levels will drop if the workforce really knows what's on our agenda, so we better not tell them everything at once (piecemeal approach).

So from the intention of management wanting to "protect" and "care about their workforce," two completely different intentions or a hidden agenda could be constructed by the workforce—those that are in listening mode and at the receiving end, and could thus lead to exactly the behavior management was originally trying to avoid, namely, reducing engagement levels and performance. If the workforce makes up their own movies in their heads about scenarios, then this actually reduces engagement levels and productivity, and even worse, this could also lead to completely wrong assumptions about what such a "hidden agenda" may or may not be about.

What if transparency was less about content (data and facts) and more about being transparent about intentions?

How would that shift conversations, and how would that shift how transparency is seen in organizations?

Those were two closing questions of a LinkedIn article that I published in 2016; questions to which I have no answers, as there is no one-size-fits-all answer to them. However, these questions have kept me on my toes since then. I would like to share some thoughts and insights that have emerged around these questions and the connections I see. Research I have come across supports, contradicts, and evokes new ideas around the multifaceted topics of transparency.

Stepping Back Before Unpacking the Benefits

Let us step back a bit and set the context for exploring transparency and its relevancy to organizations around the world. Building a healthy culture has moved up on corporate agendas over recent years and has thus grown in importance. Transparency shifts conversations that, according to Judith E. Glaser, are key to good organizational culture. Judith used to say:

> "To get to the next level of greatness depends on the quality of our culture, which depends on the quality of our relationships, which depends on the quality of our conversations. Everything happens through conversations!" (Glaser, 2014).

Every day people are having conversations in the workplace. Formal and informal conversations, conversations between colleagues (internal) and with customers and clients (external). This is all so natural. However, how natural and normal is it to actually be more intentional about what is shared in those conversations and how it is shared?

How often do we:

- Think about whether or not it is appropriate to share this piece of information?
- Consider the impact we are making on our conversation partners by sharing this with them?
- Consciously consider how we are delivering our messages? Do we listen to our counterpart or do we speak more?
- Create clarity for ourselves about how honest and open we are with our conversation partners? Are we hedging? Do we trust each other? Will there be any judgment or repercussions when I say what is truly on my mind?

When looking at the Latin origin (trans-parere -> through - appear) of the word *transparency* or *transparent* definitions such as the following can be found in dictionaries and on the internet:

"Allowing light to pass through so that objects behind can be distinctly seen."

"Easy to perceive or detect."

"Thoughts or feelings that are easily perceived."

For me, the following three words come to mind when thinking of transparency in a corporate context:

- Direction
- Clarity
- Appropriateness

Direction

This is something we, as individuals, and also companies as systems, are often trying to seek and gain more of because personal satisfaction, fulfillment, and success depend on having a clear view of the direction we are heading in. A *clear* direction is priceless. A direction that can be seen by everyone, and that can be taken, if wanted, or changed, if felt inappropriate or wrong. Such a *clear* direction helps us to move forward, or to take a break and redirect our endeavors and readjust our path(s) forward.

Clarity

Having clarity around the direction and a shared understanding of *how* to move in that direction, and why and what for, obviously are connected with this aspect of transparency. In other words, how much is shining through of what is to be achieved in a very general sense?

According to Wikipedia: "Transparency, as used in science, engineering, business, the humanities, and in other social contexts, is operating in such a way that it is easy for others to see what actions are performed. Transparency implies openness, communication, and accountability."

Openness and communication are additional key terms that can lead the way and bring more transparency into organizations. Openness and communication are, however, also the tricky elements. One has to tread carefully in the corporate world, or with absolute clarity around how *appropriate* it is to communicate openly on a particular topic. *Appropriateness* or good judgment around what is appropriate are indispensable. By proceeding with a certain level of appropriateness when sharing information, more structure, clarity, and emotional stability will emerge as a result. Structure, clarity, and emotional stability again will allow organizations to move forward in a more aligned and healthier manner, onboarding everyone who shall be onboarded. In an organizational setting it is absolutely important to have clarity around *who* can communicate *what* to *whom* and *when*. Those that are communicating need to ensure that they know who the audience is, what is the context my audience is in, and how appropriate is it for me to have this conversation.

Appropriateness

This seems to me another important aspect of transparency— especially in a corporate context. Total transparency, as research has shown, does not always have a positive impact. According to Christensen (2002) transparency and the communication embodying the latter require context and a shared understanding of meaning around what is being communicated. Knowing how much transparency is appropriate and with whom is part of the success equation when building an organizational culture with transparency as one of their pillars.

Transparency is important, yet it must present itself at the right time, in the right dose, and with the right people. Transparency is a significant success factor for organizations when establishing trust, which is vital in VUCA (V=Volatility U=Uncertainty C=Complexity A=Ambiguity) times, when changes are a constant part of organizational development. Especially then, communication needs to be open (transparent) and yet custom-tailored for the different recipients in an organization. According to Rawlins (2009) orientation and a clear sense of direction make people (individuals) and organizations (systems) move easier and swifter, *if* the message is shaped so that it primarily fulfills the need of the audience, e.g. employees, rather than the need of the sender, e.g. management (Rawlins, 2009).

One cannot speak about organizational culture without having a common understanding of what that term actually means. A brief introduction to Edgar Schein's Organizational Culture Model

(Schein, 2010) will therefore be further explored next to create that common understanding in this context here. I will use this popular model of Schein's and add the three dimensions of transparency that I feel are relevant in the discussion—**D**irection, **C**larity, and **A**ppropriateness (DCA)—to deconstruct and explain my personal take on the benefits of transparency in organizational settings.

A Brief Overview of Edgar Schein's Organizational Culture Model and How It Relates to Transparency and the Three Dimensions Direction, Clarity and Appropriateness (DCA).

There are three layers to Edgar Schein's Organizational Culture Model: assumptions at the most inner layer, values as a next layer between the inside and the outside, and finally the artifacts/symbols on the outer layer.

Assumptions Underlying assumptions that are embedded in the organizational culture are often hard to recognize.
Values Standards and Rules—how things are done here (at the company).
Artifacts/Symbols Things you can see from the outside and easily change, such as company logo, organizational structure, processes, etc.

For ease of understanding and simplicity, I often use the following terminology when talking about Organizational Culture:

The Person or Individual

Who is at the most inner layer of the model, with their very personal and individual views, assumptions, behaviors, preferences, and skills

The Role

As defined by the "system" or organization—with tasks and clear instructions on what to do and how to do it. Expectations and character traits are often assigned to the role, which are also easily projected on the person who executes the role, but are not necessarily those of the individual

The System

The company/organization where the role and the person are operating in. The context of the "system" is defined by how the company is seen and run both from the inside as well as from the outside

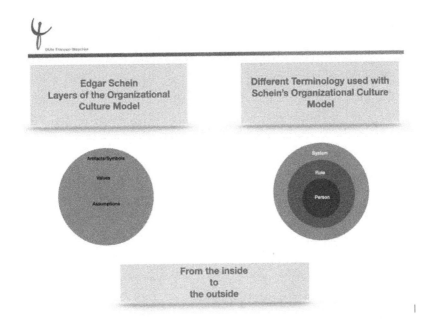

Clearly visible on the outside of the tiered model is the **System or Organization** (Artifacts & Symbols) recognizable in their company logos, the way the company is structured—degrees and levels of hierarchy, the level of standardization, the use of processes, red tape, and technology necessary to keep the "system" alive and moving.

Less clearly visible, one layer deeper, in the next tier are the **Roles** (Values) that are represented in the company, the standards—written and unwritten rules, privileges connected with certain roles, etc.—which are only visible when you are either part of the system or when you know somebody who is part of the system.

The least clarity is there when you move to the most inner tier of the model to the **Person** (Assumptions). The person is at the core, and even though the person/individual is the smallest part within the system, each person holds assumptions that influence the system. The more there is congruence from the inside to the outside the better for the entire system—less friction, more effectiveness and efficiency.

A mismatch or dissonance between the person/individual and the way they are showing up in their roles could lead to an imbalance within the ecosystem of the organization. Candid conversations about this dissonance are necessary to reestablish the balance. If avoided, this can have detrimental effects.

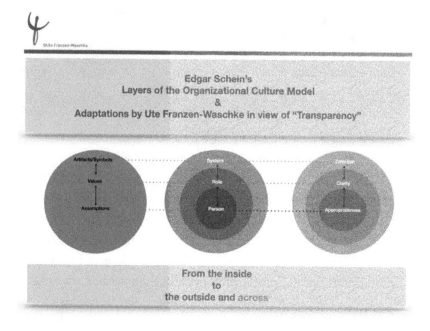

When a person (at the core of the model) does not feel in alignment with the outside layers (Role & System) and vice versa, collaboration will become difficult, and trust can disappear. Consequently, people start hiding what is truly on their mind, how they truly feel about their role, the company, etc. When behavior and assumptions (of a person/individual) are kept under the surface (by the person/individual)—or remain invisible—there is a clear lack of transparency on a personal level with a direct and immediate impact on the role and system level of the model.

Edgar and Peter Schein also expanded on this in a Q&A session in May 2019 hosted by WBECS about their book "Humble Leadership" where they said, what they called the "professional distance relationship," is based on a clear understanding of roles and systems. Both continue that organizations are advised to personalize that and to get to know their people better, i.e. to reduce the distance between the individual and the role. The roles usually are clearly defined and sustained. However, the more organizations know about the combination of the personal (person/individual) and professional individual (role), when combining both, the more sharing and participation is going to happen from the inside of the tiered model to the outside. This, however, requires an atmosphere of trust in those organizations. A willingness to open up and to be transparent beyond "the job" and "role expectations," and an honest and authentic interest in the individual on a mutual and reciprocal basis.

This call for "reducing the distance" sounds to me at the same time as a call for more transparency and openness. It's an invitation to every individual within the system to open up about *their* values, assumptions, and how *they* see *their* role(s) in the system. That of course makes each individual vulnerable within the system, if the system is not mature enough to have these kinds of open conversations. From neuroscience we know how important it is that "the I inside the WE" is seen and acknowledged (Glaser 2014). What "I" (the individual), as a part of the "system" (we), like about both the role and the system, and what "I" (the individual) feel needs improving or updating in the "system" (we), calls for higher levels of transparency and for "shining some light" on these things that have not (yet) become clearly visible, such as:

- Which direction is the system going to take?

- Where are WE (system) heading?
- Can I as the individual (I) within the system (WE) in my role comply with that? Or are there any roadblocks—dissonances of various kinds?
- Will I, my skills, and experience, still be needed in the system (WE) moving forward?

To aim at such a level of clarity and transparency does bear some risks, and, one could say knowing about the power of transparency is both relevant and important for organizations, because if not used with conscious competence, transparency can become a delicate topic and can even damage a system from the inside out (from the I to the WE or from the inner layer of the model to the outer layer of the model). Transparency can shake both the system and the people within and can cause cracks that cannot be mended so easily.

Hence for transparency to work, good relationships within the system are key. Starting from the inside out, let's take a look at a model that was created by Judith E. Glaser - the TRUST model (Glaser, 2014). The TRUST model helps individuals and organizations assess their levels of trust and looks at five different dimensions—one being transparency. Transparency as the foundation or a starter for the rest of the dimensions to develop and grow.

How Can We Foster Personal Relationships That Co-create a Shared Level of Transparency within Corporate Environments?

"The quality of our culture depends on the quality of our relationships, which depend on the quality of our conversations. Everything happens through conversation!" ~Judith E. Glaser, 2014.

How can we adapt that mantra and work toward having the necessary conversations that enable us to grow as individuals (I) and as parts of the system (WE)? By adapting that mantra, we would help the system (WE) to grow and flourish.

The individual letters of Glaser's TRUST model stand for:

T	transparency
R	relationships
U	understanding
S	shared success
T	test assumptions/truth telling

Transparency is the first letter in the model. And even though there is no hierarchy within the dimensions of this model, I personally think that transparency is something that builds a solid basis for the other dimensions to develop and expand, and really increases TRUST in a system or an organization.

Transparency

As seen in Glaser's TRUST model, this ensures that fears and threats, which might already be in the way or could get in the way in the future, are brought to the surface—are made visible. This is not an easy mission and requires individuals and organizations to be brave. Only when individuals feel safe, they will be able to open up and look at a future that might be a bit scary because it's unknown and feels uncertain (e.g. in a VUCA world).

Relationships

This is the next dimension and helps individuals to learn to listen—not to prove their own point, but to connect with the other person, who is in sending mode.

Understanding

This is where someone else stands and tries to understand their point—not necessarily to agree but to be willing to "stand under their reality" if only for a moment. That sends such a strong message showing openness to understand where my conversation partner comes from without the intention to convince them and pull them into "my corner."

Shared Success

This is the next dimension where the focus is on co-creating mutual success—success for the entire system/organization.

Testing Assumptions and Telling the Truth

This is the last, as well as a pinnacle, of all five dimensions. This dimension parallels Edgar Schein's Organizational Culture model, where at the core, assumptions reside and where the make-or-break factors for success are hidden in the individual. Without the ability to openly share what truly is on our minds, and without the ability to really listen, we will not be able to close possible reality gaps. These gaps will get in the way of the individuals and the system. Here, the highest level of transparency and trust can be reached, but only when all dimensions have been worked on and have been built up.

Conclusion

Coming back to the two questions from the beginning:

- What if transparency was less about content (data and facts) and more about being transparent about intentions?

- How would that shift conversations in organizations? And how would that shift impact how transparency as such is seen and experienced in organizations?

- And finally, why learning more about the significance and importance of transparency is so invaluable for leaders and organizations alike.

The conclusions can be summarized as follows:

- If transparency was less about content and more about intentions, leaders in general would be operating more from the inside to the outside of the models presented here.

- Leaders and organizations would put the person/the individual at the center of their attention, offering transparency with the intention to provide a sense of direction and clarity that puts neither the individual nor the system at risk.

- Transparency that comes with the right level of appropriateness and from a position of TRUST, where conversations build relationships, then those relationships build a solid basis for a great corporate culture.

That is a vantage point for both the individuals, who work in such an environment, and organizations, which strive to be successful in a VUCA world, to embark on their journey toward a healthy and sustainable organizational culture.

Shifting conversations so that leaders can adjust and leverage the different needs in a transparent system is a skill that can be learned. By honing that skill, clarity around the leaders' intentions and their impact emerge. With that clarity the leader becomes more conversationally intelligent and with that helps co-create a healthier and more sustainable place to live and to work.

Are you and your organization ready to get to the next level of greatness by using transparency as a catalyst for a healthy and sustainable organizational culture?

References

Glaser, J. E. (2014). *Conversational Intelligence: How Great Leaders Build Trust and Get Extraordinary Results*. Brookline, MA: Bibliomotion, Inc.

Schein, E. H. (2010). *Organizational Culture and Leadership*. Hoboken, NJ:Jossey-Bass.

Christensen, L. T. (2002, September 01), "Corporate Communication: The Challenge of Transparency." *Corporate Communications: An International Journal*, Vol. 7 No. 3, pp. 162-168. https://doi.org/10.1108/13563280210436772

Electronic Resources

https://en.wikipedia.org/wiki/Transparency_(behavior)

https://www.merriam-webster.com/dictionary/transparency

https://www.dictionary.com/browse/transparency

https://dictionary.cambridge.org/us/dictionary/english/transparency

https://www.wbecs.com

7

How to Transform Company Culture and Create Engagement

By Vicky Miethe
Culture Shift Creator | Coach | Consultant
Hesselager, Denmark

> "Lasting cultural change is integrated from bottom to top and you can do it in just a few days!"
> ~Vicky Miethe

I believed for many years that I was ready for and open to change. It turns out that it depends.

You have probably taken part in the process of change at work at some point. The change can have a varying scope, from introducing a new IT system, a significant organizational change, to significant turnaround projects.

When you think back to one or more change projects you have been part of, either as a decision-maker or as a staff member, what's the first thing you experienced? Today, how would you react to the same situation?

- How ready are you for change?
- When do you experience a willingness to change?

- When do you experience resistance to change?

For many years I believed that I was ready for and open to change. Today, however, I realize that my openness to change depends entirely on the change and, not least, who initiated it and how much influence I have on how to navigate the changes. If I have chosen the change myself, I experience it as challenging, yes, and also exciting and engaging.

When I experience change coming at me as a directive or some other change in circumstance, I have no say in myself (e.g., authorities, the boss, even the weather) I typically respond with reservation or direct resistance. Invite me into the design and navigation of the change early in the process, and my reaction is different. I become more open and engaged in the process.

Resistance to Change is Natural

I have asked the question "How ready are you for change?" to my colleagues, clients, and collaborators over several years. I typically get the same answer after some reflection time from the person answering.

And that is natural. Our brains are designed to ensure our survival. Literally.

The first parts of our brain have to do with survival and are highly automated. We have only minimal control over them. Our brain perceives any change as a potential threat.

So, we naturally and automatically react to imposed change with reservation and resistance. Reactive resistance to change is not new knowledge; however, it is vital to have in mind when you plan a change in your organization or team.

Your Change Strategy

I have met a lot of leaders who believe that change needs to be thought out and driven by the top of the organization.

The same leaders very often also express frustration with their beautifully designed plan that is not getting integrated throughout the organization. They describe how they have used a lot of time, energy, and resources to think the changes through. They have carefully initiated an implementation plan intending to ensure integration of the transition into the organization. Yet they find that it doesn't happen to the extent they had expected. Some are even blaming their employees for "being resistant just to be resistant."

The management has adjusted to the idea and vision during the time they have worked through the decision process. The management has adapted, influenced, and been part of the active decision of the changes.

The management then presents the employees with the decision and a plan for how to integrate the decided changes. A well-designed project, yet the employees are left with little to contribute to it, other than following the implementation plan.

These leaders follow a change strategy based on the understanding that changes are initiated and driven by the top.

We can illustrate that strategy as:

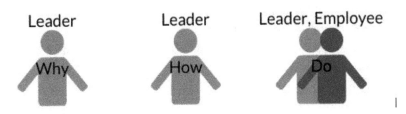

That strategy, though, does not take our neurological and psychological build into account and will result in creating unnecessary resistance.

As the decision-makers, it is so easy to forget that fundamental changes forced upon us very seldom are met with acceptance and excitement. It does not help to present the decided change with a lot of logical reasons as to why the change is necessary and useful. We need to activate the need and desire for the change and, at the same time, bypass the natural resistance to any changes.

To do that, we need to design a process that invites the employee to involvement, influencing, and contribution. In short, a process that encourages the employees to take ownership of the changes.

A change strategy that, at the same time, builds an open, co-creative, and engaged work culture in the organization.

An illustration of this strategy could look like:

Simple, isn't it?

And you can do it in just a couple of days!

How would you, your team, and organization benefit by shifting your culture effectively toward change ready, co-creative, and engaged work culture?

What if employees could start collaborating in ways that created new opportunities and developed faster and quicker agility to change when needed?

Sounds too good? It is not! It is possible, by starting from how we, as human beings, are built.

Let's look at an example of how it can be done by deconstructing a real case.

In this case, we used the Engagement Framework as a guideline for change. This framework is actively making use of the last illustrated change strategy. The framework guides us to put the relationships in the organization before objectives, which accommodates how our brains work. The Engagement Framework also entails involving employees actively throughout the process of change and, to no small extent, allowing them to run part of the process.

Doing so requires courage and confidence for most leaders. As a leader, you, in return, will gain trust, loyalty, commitment, and solutions that effectively return visible results, typically within only a short timeframe. Just as this live case.

Case History

A service company had experienced a significant drop in their brand name, a reduction evident in both their sales and their revenue. The board decided that a substantial change was needed. To help turn the company around, the board hired a new CEO.

Before the new CEO took over, the organization had a work culture with the mindset "we save as much as possible." This mindset included their after-sale support, with a focus to keep the overhead the highest in the market.

The new CEO, together with the board, wanted to change the culture to "we help for self-help." They intended to offer help and after service from the start of the relationship to help their customers to be self-reliant. The philosophy for this new company culture was that by helping from the beginning, their customers would be more satisfied, recommend the company to more, and, in the long run, take up fewer support hours.

Since "save as much as possible" was the applied understanding in the organization for several years, the new management was aware that changing the culture would be a process that required more than a managerial decision for the work culture to shift.

They involved the top leaders in the work. They entrusted all leaders, especially the team leaders, to drive the implementation and integration process and ensure that "help for self-help" was the focus in all customer interactions.

Yet, after a few months, the top management realizes that the change has not gone through.

The Call for Consultant Help

The first step in creating a sustainable process of change is knowing where to start. Successful change often begins with a study of what does/does not work, what the engagement level for the change is, and what is the degree of trust.

In this specific organization, such an investigation revealed a very high number of customer complaints, both regarding the quality of the company's performance and about their support. Thus, no single department, but the entire company needed to create a culture change. Also, the study revealed:

- The employees in customer support felt singled out as "scapegoats."
- Confidence in management throughout the company was low and extra low in customer support.
- Collaboration among employees was low, and there were both open and hidden internal conflicts.
- Employees and middle managers had, for several years, felt threatened with being fired if they did not save money and keep costs to an absolute minimum.
- There were stories that the new senior management was only out to slim down the organization and that the vision was a savings exercise in disguise. In other words, there was a general lack of trust in management.

The Actions to Set Up Ground Rules

Without first establishing a certain degree of trust between senior management and employees, including the middle managers, we would not come any further.

As humans, we build trust on sincerity and transparency, and the organization had a severe need for someone to take the first sincere steps. We, therefore, asked the new CEO to prepare to open up and show who she was as a person.

After a little personal coaching, the CEO visited all departments. She came dressed informally, without any agenda other than sharing her vision for the organization with each department specifically, as well as being open to questions and suggestions. In each department, she divulged a very personal and vulnerable experience she had had, which had significant consequences for her. Subsequently, she was open to questions.

A two-day workshop followed the tour for the entire assembled organization. This particular company chose to shut down for two days to get everyone to the same workshop. Other companies, however, have decided to meet with the organization throughout several workshops.

We designed a structured process using the Engagement Framework. We made sure to include both what works and does not work today. With all members of the organization's collective aspiration of how their ideal work culture would be, based on the new vision, the employees worked departmentally and across departments, in turn, setting up different behavioral guidelines for the company's primary stakeholders, keeping the customer as the absolute first.

Management, including both senior and middle management, worked alongside the employees to discover what their role as managers should be to give employees the best opportunity to work according to the new vision.

Each group's work was shared in plenary sessions and questioned diligently by other groups.

The two days resulted in a set of ground rules. To ensure that the engagement created at the workshop was kept alive, leadership chose to support all managers with personal coaching for a period afterward.

The Yield

After the two days, the result was:

- Consensus on the chosen changes.
- Specific behavioral rules/guidelines that ensured that stakeholders experienced the decided changes immediately.
- Trust in management. To such an extent, that other change projects in the organization have subsequently been discussed and implemented in close, open collaboration between management and employees.
- Engagement and well-being went from between 1 and 2 on a 5-point scale where 5 is the highest, to between 4 and 5. These results still hold more than six years later.
- They revealed and resolved both open and hidden conflicts.
- Better communication and collaboration within and across departments.
- Customer complaints went from seventy per day to one per quarter.
- Sick absence decreased by 85 percent
- Staff turnover decreased by 39 percent
- New ideas and suggestions rose from zero to nine per month.

- The yield is provided by the organization during a six-month follow-up evaluation of the process).

Three Critical Keys for Success with Change

Let's deconstruct what created a successful process of cultural change.

To understand the background of how we changed the culture quickly and efficiently, we need to look at the three critical keys to success in the processes of change.

Studies show that successful changes that take hold depend on the willingness of employees to change.

Willingness to change depends on the degree of:

1. Trust in management.
2. The understanding of why changes are necessary or appropriate on a personal level = motivation for change.
3. The feeling of security; a sense of what the change will mean in practice for each individual.

Let's look at the three assumptions one at a time:

Trust in Management

Confidence in management primarily depends on the quality of the relationship between managers and employees.

You can determine the confidence in management by answering these questions:

- How is communication?
- Does the manager listen to the employees?
- What is the manager's degree of credibility?

- How does what the manager says line up with the employees' perception of the managers' behavior in everyday life?
- Does the manager practice what he/she preaches?

The quality of the relationship is the cardinal point for proper management, and it is one of the areas where it pays best to invest in developing trust because confidence in the organization is readable directly on the bottom line.

The Impact of Lacking Trust

Paul J. Zak's (Director of the Center for Neuroeconomics Studies at Claremont Graduate University) recent research proves that low trust in the organization means:

- More mistakes
- More sick leave
- Less commitment
- Lower efficiency

The Influence of Trust
While high trust means:

- Better collaboration
- Fewer sick days
- Greater engagement and creativity
- High effectiveness

Therefore, concerning the change process, it is essential to include the degree of trust and then increase and reinforce it as part of the process.

Judith E. Glaser has, by way of Conversational Intelligence, discovered how to increase and maintain trust, even in challenging situations. One of the significant methods is transparency: to be open and honest and present, as well as to listen. Trust deals with relationships before the message.

In the above case, the CEO went around to all the departments. She shared a very personal and vulnerable personal experience as well as her vision, not just for the company, but also for the individual department's role in the vision. She was also open to suggestions and answered the questions she received.

The personal story made her vulnerable. She became a human being and not just a title. Most employees could see themselves in parts of her story, so she became accessible. She became perceived as "friendly" by the majority. Thus, there was greater openness to hearing what the vision was and, not least, more courage to ask questions and make suggestions—including the more critical ones.

The employees' minds opened, and they no longer saw only danger. Possibilities were now visible.

The CEO's tour of the entire organization was outstanding because it increased the level of trust. However, that alone would not have turned the mood. It was just as important to follow up on the early success—first and foremost by including and addressing the suggestions and questions posed by the employees during her tour. That's where having been heard showed. It increased both confidence and curiosity so that employees arrived at the workshop more engaged than doubtful.

Understanding Why Changes are Necessary or Appropriate = Motivation for Change

The motivation behind change is the driving force. That's what gets us to act. If a process of change is to succeed, employees must be motivated to change. Moreover, their motivation must be more potent than old habits and the fears that change quite naturally stirs up. Any change triggers a degree of concern/fear. We must step out of our comfort zones, which is always challenging.

The challenge of motivation is that what motivates one person does not necessarily motivate another to the same degree. In general, there are two primary categories of motivation:

- **"Away from" Motivation (Push)** is something we want to remove ourselves "away from." It can be anything from, for example, a poor working environment, long transport time, working with a particular person or work in a specific area.
- **"Toward" Motivation (Pull)** is something we want to achieve. For example, greater flexibility, the opportunity to organize one's working hours, more significant responsibility/promotion, or connection to a personal mentor.

Typically, most of us are "away from" motivated (80 percent) than "toward" motivated (20 percent).

Most of us, however, are best motivated by the influence of both "away from" and "toward" elements. It may sound confusing, but many of us just need to activate both before we act 100 percent wholeheartedly.

We may well be "toward" motivated in one area while we are "away from" motivated in another.

Motivation is what makes us act, and since we cannot assume that all employees and managers in the organization are motivated by the same thing, *both* "away from" *and* "toward" motivation must be included in any process of change.

In the described case, the CEO shared the vision preliminarily on her tour to each department; she shared what the vision was and why it was necessary.

We incorporated both push and pull motivation into the tasks the participants got during the workshop. We emphasized the consequences of no change on day one. The second day we worked almost exclusively with pull motivation. Strong pull motivation is influence:

to be heard and allowed to contribute.

On day one of the workshop, management had stated that this was a shared process, a process where all were equal, and each manager shared their group work with the employees. It increased trust and turned influence into substantial motivation.

The Feeling of Security = Sense of What It Will Mean in Practice for the Individual

The feeling of security is often confused with trust in management. Even though faith in the management, or rather, lack of confidence in the management, will intensify insecurity, this element is essential in and of itself.

Most are familiar with Maslow's pyramid of needs. Scientists have now shown that the pyramid contains slightly different weightings than most of us learned. While the essential needs at the apex of the pyramid still consist of food, water, etc., now, additionally, is that on *equal footing* with water and food, is the feeling of belonging and being secure—being safe.

For us to be open to engaging at all, to be creative, and to contribute effectively, we must feel safe.

Our sense of safety is challenged during any changes because changes in our environment and everyday life trigger signals and hormones that activate the "danger" center of the brain. All due to uncertainty about what our role will be in the future. If we do not address these signals quickly and efficiently, employees will respond from a state of resistance. It is not necessarily a conscious choice, but rather, chemical reactions in the brain that trigger it unless the individual is very self-aware.

Resistance to change arises because of insecurity and anxiety about: What does this mean? Can I do it?

Every change is a step out of our comfort zone. And it is, by definition, dangerous from your brain's perspective.

Dr. Andy Molinsky, Professor of Psychology from Harvard University and Professor of Organizational Behavior at Brandeis University's International Business School, has defined five blocks/challenges that we typically experience one or more of when we move outside our comfort zones:

Authenticity Challenge

1. A feeling that "this is not me at all."
2. Likeability challenge
3. A feeling or concern for "whether others still like me."

Competence Challenge

A feeling that "I'm not good enough for this, and that's apparent to others." Often followed by a sense of embarrassment or shame.

Resentment Challenge

A strong feeling that "it should not be necessary for me to do this," followed by a sense of frustration and anger.

Morality Challenge

A feeling that this behavior is not "right" and the concern and guilt this may cause.

In the process of change, one must be proactive in minimizing the danger signals, both with clear and precise information, as well as with practical examples of the effect of each—and with high responsiveness to the employees' thoughts, feelings, and ideas.

The most effective way to do this in practice is by actively involving employees in the process. With open, accepting information and communication before, during, and after, and the ability and willingness to listen.

In our case, we designed the whole process to minimize the sense of "danger" and actively involve the employee throughout the workshop:

- The CEO's personal tour of the company kick-started a willingness to listen to the employees, which lowered the sense of danger for the majority of employees before the workshop.
- The design of the workshop ensured the employees and the leaders were on equal footing. Employees defined the behavioral ground rules toward essential stakeholders, including the customers. This actively involved and increased the employees' influence on how they conducted the change in their everyday work.

If change is carried out with these three elements in mind, while the person(s) facilitating the processes are accepting, listening to create connection, and open to adjustments along the way, even a significant change in practice could be accomplished within a few days—often by the employees themselves.

The role of leadership, then, is to follow up, create a framework that supports the employees' efforts, and continue to dialogue with them afterward.

Summary

What the CEO Did to Make the Change Happen

First, the CEO dared to show her most vulnerable side. In consideration of the nature of what she shared, I will not repeat the story here other than to say she revealed that she was a human being with faults and defects like everyone else. And that she learned from her mistakes. Also, employees noted that she took the time to meet them all and listen to what they had to say, even when they criticized her and the vision directly.

Her tour of all departments both primed the employees for the workshop and made it visible to them that she was honest and human, that she wanted to hear their side, and was open to being influenced. She showed transparency that created greater security while increasing trust in both herself and the top management.

The CEO's tour changed the attitude about her for the majority of employees. She had made the first step in rebuilding trust.

The Design of the Workshop

Employees were in the center of the workshop. Based on the new vision and examples from everyday life offered by the employees themselves, what worked, and what did not, soon became apparent—from the employees themselves. We made sure to activate the motivation for "something to be changed." And we ensured we covered both "away from" and "toward" motivation during the workshop.

The employees' defined what was required in the way of factual actions and daily behaviors, thus strengthening their sense of security through their influence.

The fact is that, in this, management openly laid it out for the employees to define the necessary behavioral changes and concurrently agreed that those also applied to the management, which contributed to both increasing trust and security.

The management had set up a wish scenario for how far the process would take them.

The process surpassed the management scenario on all parameters. The employees even suggested changes that were more far-reaching than management had thought possible.

The follow-up personal coaching ensured that the management did not fall back into old habits and that they got the tools they needed to help the employees stick to the new guidelines.

The Outcome

The result the company achieved was not just short-term. At the time of writing, it has been more than six years, and today the company is considered one of the best in their industry.

They have established a culture of change-readiness—which they now see as entirely natural—which supports suggestions and input from both management and employees. When things need to be changed, the employees are actively involved. Not necessarily all of them, but both management and employees get invited to participate, and task forces across affected areas join and are responsible for implementation.

The CEO says that her job today is to have and keep hold of the vision in the long-term and to pave the way so that managers and employees have the opportunity to live it. She finds that employees speak to each other across departments and invite collaboration and communication themselves when one or more people experience challenges.

Her final remark is:

"Implementing cultural change based on the employees' input was the best thing we've done. Our success today would not have been possible if we had not cooperated across hierarchy and department. Today it is our foundation stone, and we would not survive without it."

Literature and Notes:

Trust Factor: The Science of Creating High-Performance Companies by Paul J. Zak – Director of the Center for Neuroeconomic Studies ISBN: 9780814437667. Published by Amacom, 2017.

Conversational Intelligence – How Great Leaders Build Trust and Get Extraordinary Results by Judith E. Glaser. ISBN: 978-I-937134-67-9. Published by Bibliomotion, Inc., 2014.

In Search of Honor: Lessons from Workers on How to Build Trust by Adele B. Lynn. ISBN: 0-9664084-4-6. Published by Bajon House Publishing, 1998.

Reach: How to Build Confidence and Step Outside Your Comfort Zone by Dr. Andy Molinsky. ISBN: 978-0-241-25132-4. Published by Penguin Random House Group, 2017.

8

Case Study: Agile Project Room

By Christian Délez
Agile Project Leader | Coach | Facilitator
Neuchâtel, Switzerland

> "The most exciting breakthroughs of the twenty-first century will not occur because of technology but because of an expanding concept of what it means to be human."
> ~ John Naisbitt

The Employee's Morning

As usual, Martin wakes up and does his morning routine before going to work. He wonders if there will be again those long meetings where only a few speak, and no big ideas or issues get spoken. Maybe there will be another management announcement or measure he doesn't understand as he feels disconnected with the leadership. Martin sets himself in "just another workday" mode and goes to work. He doesn't feel engaged.

On the way to work, Martin notices the colorful sky and thinks,

"We will see how the day goes..." As usual Martin will read and address the pile of emails. For sure, he will need to write emails to "cover his ass!" to avoid future potential blaming. Apart from that, he may have a bit of time to get some real work done.

A Safe Space

Martin arrives to work, grabs his mug, and moves to the coffee machine to get a good morning coffee. He meets Julia who asks, "Have you heard about that agile project room stuff? Our team has to go to the other building after lunch to get an introduction." They both make some hypothesis about it and then go check their emails.

After lunch, each member of the team moves to a room in the next building, a room they've never before experienced. They arrive in a large room, big enough to contain four times as many people. They look small inside that room, furnished with a few workstations, a big table with a seat for everyone, and empty walls with some signs on them.

The team manager says, "Welcome to our new agile project room where all the collaboration for our product development team will take place starting today. I present to you, Sarah, our coach who will guide us through the process." The team members talk with one another, some smiling, some waiting to see what comes next and no one saying anything to the larger group.

Sarah the coach starts explaining the purpose of this agile room. "This room is only for you, the project team building this product. You will collaboratively work here all together on a regular basis. One challenge that teams have is how to handle difficult conversations effectively in times of uncertainty, turbulence, and when the unexpected happens. I will help you acquire the needed human skills to go through every conversation with ease, such that you can build a great product and have fun with your colleagues."

Sarah shares a personal, emotional story where she had a really hard time with some work colleagues for a long period of time and what she learned from it. She assured the team she will hold the space for such difficult conversations and keep what happens in this room private with the team.

The Agile Project Room

Figure 1: Agile Project Room

The room has several areas:

- A collaborative area with tables formed in an open square or rectangle and enough chairs for everyone. In that area, team meetings and discussions take place.

- A huge screen next to the collaborative area where any needed document, picture or resource can by shown.

- Shared workstations connected to the team online document library where several team members can collaborate together on documents on big screens.

- Isolated small tables for work in subgroups.

- A wall "Team rules & info." The rules of conduct that the team will define with the coach will by posted there. Information like holidays or absence map, and a personal information page per team member will also be on that wall.

- A wall "Our product." This wall is all about the product the team is building. It contains information like the shared vision of the team, what the product will be, the road map to achieve this vision, and the main capabilities of the product, all shared in a visual format.

- Several flipcharts for spontaneous and ongoing collaboration and co-creation sessions.

For the rest of the afternoon, Sarah the coach lets the team members discuss among themselves the opportunities they see of the agile project room.

Handle Any Conversations

On the morning of day two, Sarah the coach starts with a team coaching session. "Today the focus is on you as a team and as each individual. We will define your team rules, and we will get to know one another better. We will also learn how to have better conversations, including the difficult ones." They all meet in a large circle of chairs and learn to do a check-in (reference: Google Aristotle psychological safety Amy Edmondson teaming), which allows each person to state how she/he feels and better connect with the team members for the day.

Figure 2: Coaching Session

They all go through several immersive exercises in which they learn about the power of words, and how to better understand the meaning of words somebody else uses. They learn to lessen the use of words that disengage collaboration and use more words that increase collaboration and engagement.

Martin doesn't feel comfortable speaking up in the circle. However, he shares some personal feelings and stories. He is surprised by what he hears from his colleagues; personal stories he didn't know about. Some stories resonate in Martin's head and he now better understands some colleagues; he even feels more connected to them.

Sarah the coach tells them they will do similar sessions in the future to learn, enhance, and sustain their conversational practices.

Team Rules

In the afternoon, Sarah the coach helps the team to develop its organizational rules. Sarah tells them, "We will define together some organizational rules on how we organize the work and how we collaborate with one another. One big change is there will be zero emails between us—every conversation takes place in this room, and small chat in the chat tool. Every decision takes place in this room and is immediately documented in the shared document library. I will guide you the first few times, then you will know how to make it on your own."

A conversation starts with the team and how this could even work. They play with some scenarios using the new rules.

The next item on the organizational level is to have personal data for everyone working on the team. Sarah the coach facilitates an exercise that creates a one-page datasheet per team member called the Personal Map. Each team member draws a map with personal information and points of interest unknown to others that help people connect and develop a relationship-before-tasks attitude. The map also identifies capabilities, skills, and experiences that could be useful to the workplace.

They make a presence and holidays map on the wall in order to know for weeks to come who is available when for the project or if a member is away for several days. They plan some fixed days where they will meet in the agile project room.

Project Vision and Road Map

On day three, they all meet in the agile project room. The focus today is on the product the team is building together. Using the learning of day one coaching session, the team works on crafting the product vision statement. Sarah the coach helps them to elevate the conversation such that the vision statement becomes appealing and clearly sharp. The discussions are intense, full of emotions, and the resulting vision statement motivates the team to move forward.

In the afternoon, the team, inspired by the vision, creates the road map of the product. Now that they are aligned with a common vision, they find it an easy task to draw a road map that sequences the product development phases. They add major milestones and deliverables. The team hangs these outcomes in large paper format on the "Product wall." There is room on the wall for more to come in the coming weeks. The team is happy; many are smiling. They end the day by a small celebration ritual to acknowledge what they have done.

The Power of the Flipchart

On day four, Sarah the coach provides the opportunity for the team to experience co-creation on flipcharts. She makes two groups, each one at a small table with a flipchart. Group 1 gets the task to draw an overview of the product. Group 2 gets the task to draw the user experience a customer of the product will have.

At the beginning, members of each group sit and discuss on their own. After a while, Sarah the coach goes to group 1, asks some discovery questions and starts to draw on the flipchart what she understands them to say. She then asks the group if her drawing is correct. Jim, a group member, has comments. Sarah hands him the pen, and Jim stands up and starts drawing and explaining. Then Alice speaks from the table and makes comments. Sarah hands her another pen. Alice stands up, takes the pen, and starts drawing and explaining. After some minutes, all five members of this group are standing up in front of the flipchart co-creating a view of the product. You cannot tell who draws which part as the pens move quickly from hand to hand. The group members use what they learned during day one about how to converse for co-creation. You can hear members asking powerful questions, making proposals without attachment, and checking for understanding with one another. What you don't hear is "it is wrong" or "it doesn't work."

Martin is part of group 1 and feels good during this session. He draws some sketch on the flipchart and his colleagues' comment, add, and ask questions about it. He discovers some aspects of the product he didn't know. He thinks about other sessions he could do that would provide him insights and data really fast about some of his tasks.

Figure 3: Power of Flipchart

Sarah the coach moves on to the second group, repeats the process and the same behavior can be observed in group two. Both groups co-create their outcome. You can feel engagement and full presence. Sarah reminds them to take a break. Afterward, the groups continue and easily finish their tasks before lunch. Each group takes pictures of their flipchart outcomes and stores these in the shared electronic document library. This will be the way to store and share outcomes of co-creation sessions in the project.

Questions Space

In the afternoon of day four, Sarah the coach launches a Q&A session. "What else can we do to work better here?" She builds on the openness and psychological safety developed in the morning. The members explore new territories; they invent the next steps in how they want to improve.

Martin takes the courage to make a proposal he was thinking about for a long time. He is surprised that two other colleagues feel the same and enhances his proposal, which gets attention from the whole team. Martin feels empowered and engaged.

At the end of the afternoon, the team has a list of improvements they want to implement to get better results more easily. Each team member identifies with the changes the team has agreed to make. Each team member feels responsible for the improvement outcome.

Learning and Reflections

On day five, there are no team sessions planned. As proposed by Sarah the coach, Martin uses the day to reflect on his learnings and experiences of the week. Martin recaps his week:

- On day one, Martin felt afraid when called to go into an unknown room and then Martin felt surprised to be part of a new experiment for project and teamwork.
- The project room is a space dedicated to the project team with walls of information (team and product) and the needed infrastructure to co-create and innovate.

- There will be no emails between team members anymore. All will be done in the room in collaboration sessions and via the chat tool. Martin loves that; he is sick of writing emails that get wrongly interpreted and generate more work instead of solutions.

- On day two, Martin learned how to better communicate in a team context; how to process tensions and conflicts, how to speak out fears, how to propose crazy and innovative ideas. He still does not fully feel comfortable about this new way of working and conversing and is happy that Sarah the coach will be supporting him for a while.

- On day three, the team defined the product vision and its road map.

- The organizational and behavioral rules for the project team have been defined.

- All information hangs on the wall of the agile project room.

- On day four, Martin experienced the power of a co-creation session with flipcharts. He felt creative and innovative.

- He experienced a team Q&A session in an environment of trust that generated new opportunities for better teamwork.

A Month Later

A month later, Martin reflects on the changes that did occur. He loves the production pipeline description wall they created; one wall of the project room describes phase by phase the steps of production (pipeline) of their product. The description is based on flipcharts, with colorful drawings and Post-it notes as well as other papers like one-pagers stuck to the wall. They named each phase, each step. They defined naming schemes for each artifact; they now have a product dictionary. They now have every product production discussion in front of the pipeline wall, and this brings clarity.

Martin is happy to see Sarah the coach every week when she comes to coach the team in order to improve the interaction between them and discuss any issues and struggles they have. Martin feels he could never have those breakthroughs without the coach facilitating the conversations. He sees some of the team members who may potentially do the job in the future.

Martin finds the team rhythm to be good; they meet in the project room every two or three days depending on their needs, and they adapt dynamically from week to week. He likes this clarity between the workdays in plenum and the workdays alone where he can concentrate on specific tasks.

They did revisit the team rules and made some changes and improvements. Martin is happy that these are not static. He noticed how fast things are evolving from one week to another.

Martin had several flipchart sessions with some of his colleagues. He is amazed by the outcomes. He now has a powerful tool to gather facts and knowledge when tackling complex ambiguous tasks.

Conclusion

Martin is a happy employee. He feels he belongs to his project, team, and company. He knows personal stories about each team member and that helps him understand everyone and engage in conversations that increase collaboration and innovation. Martin knows that every challenge can be spoken. He knows that the team will find the solution as they regularly co-create in the agile project room. It is simple, it is a place where his team can experiment and find solutions to their complex problems.

Martin goes home in the evening, looking forward to the next day of productively working with his peers in a friendly relationship atmosphere. Martin thinks he is part of a great company.

9

How TRUST Makes for a Safer World

By Karin Ovari

Safety Leader & Team Creator | Future Human Connection Designer | Psychological Safety Aficionado
Newburgh, Scotland

> "To get to the next level of greatness depends on the quality of the culture, which depends on the quality of the relationships, which depends on the quality of the conversations." ~ Judith E. Glaser

Inside high-reliability organisations (HROs) such as oil and gas, nuclear, transport, construction, health systems etc., safety is often "assumed" as the number one priority or core value—although when push comes to shove, production usually takes precedence.

Well, so they say!

There is a conflict or tension between what "should be" and the need to "get the job done."

In my eighteen-plus years of experience coaching individuals, teams, and developing "cultures of safety" within HROs, many people prefer to take the safe road. So why don't they?

What drives a culture of safety or a safety culture—is there a difference?

Almost all organisations have a safety culture, the question is "where on the culture maturity ladder do they live?"

A culture of safety is one in which safety plays a vital role. Because safety is such a complex phenomenon, it is not enough just to add, "And be safe."

Acceptance that a culture of safety is good for business, not just by reducing accidents but also for production and, therefore, financially, is crucial. One way a culture of safety pays off is as the levels and quality of communication improves so does TRUST, which has a positive effect in all areas of the business.

An influential culture of safety is good for business and has its financial rewards.

Having completed many safety culture programs and assessments, communication failures are cited as a critical source of problems for organisations. Having a definitive focus on improving communication can only result in improved performance at all levels.

What is a Culture of Safety?

Many will describe this as "the way we do things around here," which of course is how many organisational cultures describe their culture in one way or another.

Professor Patrick Hudson describes the Hudson Safety Maturity Ladder (see image 1) as an evolutionary ladder that plots the development of an organisation's safety culture. Each level has distinct characteristics and is a progression from the previous level. The range runs from the pathological, reactive, calculative, on to the proactive, and then the final stage of generative.

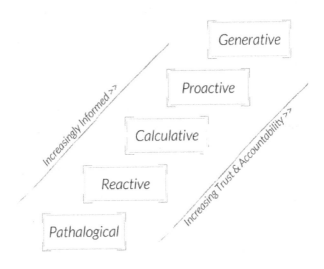

Image 1—Hudson safety culture maturity ladder

Each level of the ladder is defined to some degree as follows:

Pathological safety culture: the business drivers are seen as most important and will only do enough not to get caught by the regulators—it's a tick box exercise—and safety is considered a problem of the worker.

Reactive safety culture: As the name suggests, these organisations react to safety only after incidents occur, which is taken seriously at the time. We often see wide pendulum swings between productivity and safety at this stage.

Calculative safety culture: This level is all about data and the collection of lagging indicators. They are driven by numbers and a top-down approach, albeit safety is taken seriously. Safety expectations are imposed, and we often see safety system fatigue.

Proactive safety culture: Here, we start to see workforce involvement in what proper safety looks like and how it feels. Lagging indicators are still relevant as well as leading indicators. Behaviour and team involvement become an essential part of the safety conversation puzzle. Improved performance and higher accountability are on the rise.

Generative safety culture: "This is how we do business around here" with the perception that safety is part of the organisation's DNA with all areas of the business benefiting. Often these organisations are characterised by a state of chronic unease to ward off complacency.

Many organisations sit somewhere between levels 2 and 3, with many moving to level 4. However, very few are at level 5. To become a truly generative organisation, it has to have the aspiration and skills to get there. Once all the box-ticking exercises (referring to levels 2 and 3 in particular) are complete the only way to move forward is to deepen TRUST.

The model implies that for an organisation to become generative, it requires an increasingly informed environment, which in turn increases TRUST and accountability. Of course, systems and processes are foundational to building robust safety systems.

The focus of this chapter is on the more complicated human emotion of TRUST and understanding what conversations will get you there.

One might say it lies in the degrees of trust.

- Trust to speak up.
- Trust that my team and manager have my back.
- Trust that my team and manager can trust me.
- That our systems will work.

Let's Look at TRUST from the Dimension of Emotion.

When we say "I trust or don't trust" a person, thing or event, we often do this from a moral stance. However, TRUST, in many ways, is the best inbuilt *Risk Assessment* tool we have, and without it, we would do very little in life.

Let's think about that in a little more detail.

You are a member of a frontline working team/crew, and you all get on pretty well, and for the most part, the work gets done on time and in a reasonably safe manner. But, you know that shortcuts are taken and often by a particular team member. Is it your responsibility to say or do something about it? In your heart, you know it is not right according to the standards of the organisation's safety culture, but...

- You don't want to upset your mate.
- What are the ramifications for you if you do?
- What "uncomfortable" conversation might ensue?
- You are not comfortable with what might be a confrontation.
- What if you stopped the job and upset the job just because, after all, no one is getting hurt, and we have deadlines to reach?
- The supervisor is antsy at the moment.
- You "like" the person, they are good fun, and you don't want to upset them, and so on...

You know where I am going with this because we have all been there. So, we let it slide, and not just this time, either. You become more and more uncomfortable as time passes.

Today you are promoted, and you are now that person's supervisor and responsible for the overall safety of the team and operation. Your safety responsibilities and accountability have just increased exponentially.

How do you deal with your "mate" who you now have to manage?

What Just Happened to TRUST?

As my other mentor, Dan Newby, states in his book *The Unopened Gift: A Primer in Emotional Literacy:*

> "We have traditionally understood trust from a 'moral' perspective, meaning it had to do with our 'goodness' or 'badness' as human beings. While you are free to use this interpretation, it is more useful to think of trust, particularly from a safety perspective, as a 'risk assessment tool' based on sincerity, reliability, competence, and capacity."

Capacity is often the missing link—think back to our story above—what is missing in your assessment of TRUST in that scenario?

Mostly *capacity* refers to any job/task/work not completed toward a common standard of time, energy, money, resources, procedure, which then elevates risk.

Often people are most sincere, rarely does someone get up in the morning and think, "Excellent. Another day to do harm in any way." People turn up for the job and based on the mere fact they are employed come with some level of competence. So, we assume some level of trust exists.

Interestingly, trust is not just about other people. We have our self-assessment of trust, and we evaluate or judge others, groups, systems, and processes and safety in terms of that trust judgment. And that trust will determine our willingness to interact with others.

So effectively, we are saying that without trust, it would be almost impossible to have relationships, create safe environments, or have the right conversation at the right time to move towards a safer world.

So How Do We Develop TRUST in High-Reliability Organisations?

> "Contrary to popular belief, cultivating a high-trust culture is not a 'soft' skill—it's a hard necessity. Put another way; it's the foundational element of high performing organisations."
> ~Stephen M. R. Covey

In a 2015 Safe Work Australia publication, Dr. Sharron O'Neill, Ms. Karen Wolfe and Dr. Sasha Holley wrote that leading safe and healthy work requires five elements:

1. **Trust**—welcoming bad news, actively and consistently prioritising safety and wellbeing to demonstrate it is a primary organisational goal.

2. **Communication**—promoting cooperation, inspiring compliance, fostering group goals, and providing individualised support to foster quality interactions between managers and workers.

3. **Achieving the achievable**—recognising the factors that can be changed at each level and implementing as many safety defences as possible within their sphere of influence.

4. **Expertise and skills**—having a sound understanding of the industry and business to be able to "ask the essential questions."

5. **Visible leadership**—being "on the ground," "getting out and looking around," not to police the workforce, but to get to know the business, the sites, the people, and to lead by example.

Part of the EY Why Should I Trust You? A Fresh View of HSE report, they considered the above research, the existing safety culture models, as well as business literature on strategy, performance, and culture.

They suggest there are two fundamental drivers of organisational and safety outcomes: trust and knowledge. Their research also indicates that these are the most effective and self-sustaining.

To support that they designed a simple representation of their simple Plus One concept:

- Build shared trust.
- Enable knowledge flow.
- Seek alignment.

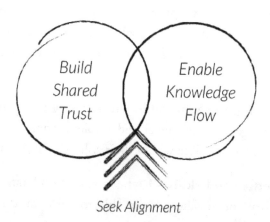

Seek Alignment

EY Plus One Concept

> "...unless the mistrust of the workforce can be overcome then even the most well-intentioned and sophisticated management initiatives will be treated with cynicism and undermined."
> ~ Professor Neil Gunningham and Darren Sinclair

These examples are just the tip of the iceberg when it comes to research on what it takes to have a sustainable culture of safety and what is obvious TRUST plays a vital role.

My humble view is that they are all missing a vital component—the conversation.

What Type of Conversations Do We Need to Have to Build TRUST?

The reason I became a Conversational Intelligence Certified Coach (C-IQ) is that I believed there is a better way to have candid conversations. Which was apparent during my many years spent at the frontline in highly hazardous environments working teams and the not so successful "safety conversation."

The best way for me to describe how to move forward and begin the journey to improving conversations to build TRUST for safety cultures is by sharing how I use our tools. To help foster and nurture the ideas from within the room on what defines the building blocks of trust and psychological safety (and that is a whole other chapter for another time).

When working with teams, I often take a temperature check of the mood in the room by using a version of what we (C-IQ coaches) call our Conversational Dashboard™. I then take attendees on a journey of neuroscience and explain what is happening inside us during the different stages, with the big question around how do we build TRUST.

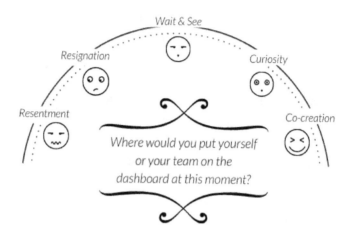

Mood Dashboard Check-in

Asking people where they live on this dashboard and what would it take to move one step along it often comes down to TRUST. I use polls to extract this excellent information, and here is an example output from a recent round table discussion on What Does Safety Mean to You?

Safety is TRUST that everyone in the team can speak up, openly share what is on their mind, and how they feel. Having TRUST that I will not be punished for being like I am or sharing my ideas. True safety must include TRUST.
~ Summary of a round table discussion on What Does Safety Mean to You? June 30, 2020

Then I reveal what else is on the dashboard, like peeling back the layers of an onion.

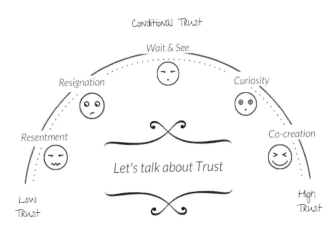

Trust Levels Visible

Robust conversations around what is happening inside us continue with many aha moments. The conversation moves from what it takes to move from Protect Mode (low trust) to Partner Mode (high trust) and everything in between.

What happens when there is a condition of low trust when we do not have enough experience with someone to evaluate his or her sincerity, reliability, competence, and capacity? Trust is a skill and competence and thus can be learned, practised, and improved.

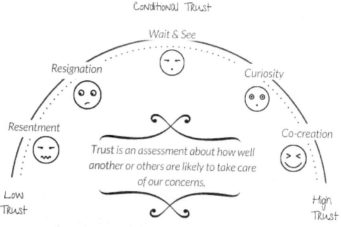

Conditional Trust

Wait & See

Resignation

Curiosity

Resentment

Co-creation

Trust is an assessment about how well another or others are likely to take care of our concerns.

Low Trust

High Trust

It can involve all or some of the following assessments
Sincerity, Competence, Reliability, Capability

TRUST Explanation

We then move on to establishing the foundations of trust, and in our C-IQ world, we discuss the elements of priming for TRUST— TRUST is something we can learn and evolve beyond pure emotional instinct and reaction.

What Are the Basics of TRUST?

T - Transparency—we create a safe environment to both share success and fears. The impact of our words matters; it is where we shift from protection to partnership. We collectively address threats and concerns.

R - Relationships—we create rapport and prime our conversations for mutual success with openness and respect. We listen to connect.

U - Understanding—we are all observers of our worlds and the only way to see their world is by stepping into the other person's shoes. We listen to understand.

S - Shared Success—let's paint a picture of shared collective success and lower our attachments to being right. We listen to co-create and open possibilities.

T-Test Assumptions & Truth-Telling—we must tell the truth with sincerity, respect, and care; we identify the reality gaps. We listen to close the gaps.

> "Without trust, it would be impossible to have relationships, create organisations, make requests, or accept promises from other people. If we do not have a high enough level of trust, we will not board an aeroplane, buy a product, or accept a job. There are very few activities we can undertake in life that do not have a dimension of trust involved." ~ Dan Newby

Conversational Intelligence can pave this road with gold, particularly if you are looking for ways to develop your capacity in becoming a generative organisation.

We are fortunate to have the very unique TRUST Catalyst Tool™, which can be a starting position in helping you to develop the levels of conversations that build the trust required to create a sustainable culture of safety. And, an alternative, the more traditional safety culture analysis.

The tool provides you with a snapshot of behaviours and conversations that are driving trust or eroding trust in your workplace. This tool can be used with a few people or with thousands of people to determine what actions you can take to elevate TRUST at work.

Conclusion

Well, what can I say? We have been on quite a journey through this chapter, and I hope that it has raised your curiosity as to how you might build upon the trust in your organisation, team or community.

Many authors agree that *trust* is the foundation of an active safety culture. It is possible to develop and cultivate a culture of safety within your organisations by building trust between employees, supervisors, and managers. In turn, this leads the workforce to exhibit more positive safety behaviours, like reporting near misses and challenging unsafe acts, resulting in fewer occupational injuries and better organisational performance, not just safety.

There is a significant difference between someone "believing safety is important" and "being a safety leader" and it all comes down to the conversations we have for building TRUST to pave the way for a safer world. ~ me.

References

Glaser, J. E. (2016). *Conversational Intelligence: How Great Leaders Build Trust and Get Extraordinary Results.* Routledge.

Newby, D., & Watkins, C. (2019). *The Field Guide to Emotions: A Practical Orientation to 150 Essential Emotions.* Verlag nicht ermittelbar.

Newby, D., & Núñez, L. (2017). *The Unopened Gift: A Primer in Emotional Literacy.* Daniel Newby.

"Safety Culture and Leadership" by Professor Patrick Hudson. (n.d.). Retrieved from https://www.safeworkaustralia.gov.au/media-centre/safety-culture-and-leadership-professor-patrick-hudson

EY.com/Publications//Why Should I Trust You a Fresh Look at HSE Culture.pdf
https://www.ey.com/Publication/vwLUAssets/EY-why-should-i-trust-you-a-fresh-look-at-hse-culture/$FILE/EY-a-fresh-look-at-hse-culture.pdf

Safework Australia Publication – "Performance Measurement, Incentives and Organisational Culture: Implications for Leading Safety and Healthy Work."
https://www.safeworkaustralia.gov.au/system/files/documents/1703/performance-measurement-incentives-organisational-culture.pdf

10

Case Study: Co-creation in Practice

By Vicky Miethe,
Tanja Murphy-Ilibasic, Sonja Vlaar
European C-IQ Collective Member Coaches

> "We, as humans, are social beings and the feeling of social security is of equal importance to us as other basic necessities such as food or shelter." ~The Authors

When we engage with others in conversations that influence our minds, hearts, and spirits, we are co-creating. This article is a case study of a co-creative process between professional coaches and illustrates how easily stumbling blocks can arise, even for those acutely aware of the challenges.

Here we are exploring the dynamics that ensued during such a process between and among coaches who all share a background and certification in the late Judith E. Glaser's Conversational Intelligence (C-IQ). The setting was our 2018 inaugural live mastermind gathering of the European C-IQ Collective in Bavaria, Germany.

Our collective co-created a virtual community using communication platforms such as Slack and Zoom videoconferences. We commit to meet once every two weeks. Since having co-created and bonded in Bavaria, we were able to easily adapt to the virtual venue and also invite new members to the community.

Our Goal as the European C-IQ Collective

- Showcase/promote the value of C-IQ for individuals, companies, and organizations within Europe.
- Grow and sustain our professional learning and application of C-IQ.
- Support each other as a professional community.
- And, last but not least, to enable collaboration and cooperation across borders and languages.

Setting Up the Exercise

The program on the second day was all about revisiting C-IQ tools in subgroups. Each subgroup consisted of four members wishing to explore a specific C-IQ tool to deepen not only our understanding of it but also to identify how to potentially incorporate it more extensively in our working practices. The focus of this article is on our own subgroup and the dynamics that ensued during the co-creative process.

We four professional coaches have an extensive accumulated wealth of experience in diverse methodologies, including C-IQ. Three of us were based directly within Europe and had been instrumental in the creation of the collective. The final member of the group was an American coach who had welcomed the opportunity to explore C-IQ concepts and approaches in greater depth with like-minded peers. Having all voluntarily selected to focus on this specific tool and sharing similar interests, we were very enthusiastic to engage with each other.

Once we had set ourselves up in a separate room, we began to discover that our mutual lack of knowledge in how to use a tool in practice was the first hurdle to overcome. Discussion was stilted, creativity low, and energy was draining away fast. We could all sense the growing disappointment and frustration within the group: some of us had expected more from our group process. Was this really all we had to share with each other about this tool?

As the silence began to grow and restlessness became prevalent, some of us began to suspect that the tool itself was simply too academic, leading to doubts on whether the time to explore it further was being wisely invested. We were all stuck in the reflection of our own professional acting. At this point, the mutual focus was still on sharing existing knowledge, of which there was little at hand.

The Turning Point

Relief from this feeling of being stuck came when one of us picked up a marker and started facilitating the group process by drawing a landscape on the flipchart, thus clearly visualising the emotional impact of each question within the tool on a scale of 1-10 and illustrating where both fear and trust lay. By making this experience explicit, the nature of the experience "unfolded" and shifted from "how to understand the tool and its use with a client" to "how to use it ourselves in the here and now." Having completed this for herself, she asked each of us to visualise our own personal landscape on the flipchart.

It was at this point that we all moved from sharing existing knowledge to a process of creativity and co-creation. From here on, the energy in the group changed dramatically, and we had a lively discussion about the intent and impact of starting a conversation with the dichotomy of trust and fear. From this discussion we discovered that, at the very least, three variables greatly impact the gut feeling of our state of mind:

- Personal drives, values, and aspirations.
- The quality of the relationship.
- The personal assessment of someone else.

What also became clear is that visualising a model is a path forward when the group dynamic process has become stuck; drawing is a way of visualisation that is very helpful in gaining more clarity about the personal instincts or characteristics that are embedded in each of us.

Impact of the Co-creating Process

By working together as a subgroup, we gained a better understanding of each other and shared our learning in an energising exchange with the support of further visualisations.

Co-creating a process, a development or solving a challenge is at any time the best way to utilize all the strengths and potential at hand.

For this co-creation to work effectively, there needs to be a clear agreement on what the group or team is trying to accomplish. In our case, it was to better understand how to use a C-IQ tool that none of us was well acquainted with and had not really used before.

From the outset, a certain degree of trust within the group or team is paramount. Otherwise, our brains and energy will be focused on our social interaction instead of on the actual task at hand. That is because we, as humans, are social beings and the feeling of social security is of equal importance to us as other basic necessities such as food or shelter. That is one of the newest findings neuroscientists have recently been able to identify, using new techniques and research methods.

In our case, trust had already been established both prior to our live event, during the many digital conference calls over the previous year, and also on the initial days of the event itself.

Co-creating entails being willing to listen to each other, being open to be influenced by ideas and opinions of others, and by being willing to stay curious of what the other people in the group think coupled with the intention of what is actually being said. Moreover, asking deeper, clarifying questions (in C-IQ terminology, we call this Double-Clicking) are key to being sure we have genuinely understood what others are trying to convey. In short, we should lock away our assumptions, including the one about us knowing how to ask questions for clarification.

When structured correctly, co-creating also deepens the level of trust between the involved parties. This again deepens the communication and co-creative process, thus allowing a positive spiral of trust and partnering to evolve.

A further puzzle piece of co-creating entails "holding the space," particularly when frustrations arise with each other or the processes.

In our own case study, we held the space for each other by all remaining at the task even when doubts started to emerge. A little later, when a misunderstanding threatened to derail the positive dynamics within the group, by holding the space we were able to explore what had actually taken place and the emotional impact this was having; we could uncover the intent behind certain actions rather than allow ourselves to be trapped within the initial impact of them; and we were able to re-establish and even grow the level of trust between each other.

This does not mean to say that there was no discomfort during this process. Indeed, there was. It simply illustrates the mutual desire to invest the effort in building our relationship and to withstand any unpleasant moments, rather than prematurely abandoning all that had been achieved.

The highly unexpected outcome of our whole exercise was the creation of an entirely new tool, that we named the Landscape Model. None of us could have imagined at the outset that working with one of our lesser-used C-IQ tools would lead to such creativity. Our appreciation of Judith E. Glaser's original tool and the value of its application was first fully realised whilst we were creating a new, complementary approach.

Summary: What is Co-creation?

We hope that this case study has succeeded in providing you with some practical examples of how we co-create within our own community. Our own understanding of the co-creation process has been captured below:

- Co-creating is hardwired into our DNA.
- Co-creating is about working together with others in a manner that provides mutual support and recognises the value we each bring to the table. This is a fundamental basis for building a strong community.
- Co-creating is sharing ideas, listening without judgment, and developing ideas together with others. In this case study, we shared how we overcame a stumbling block in the group dynamic process, giving way to the co-creation of the new Landscape Model.
- Co-creation catalyzes growth and provides relationships and communities with shared meaning.

- Co-creation is not something that suddenly happens, it is a process and it is normal that the roads of co-creation are paved with bumps, frustration, and often, ultimately, break-throughs. If we trust in the relationship, its richness has the potential to overcome challenging or difficult moments during our interactions.

- We are social beings. The need for co-creation is essential to our wellbeing and growth.

- Co-creation grows trust and deepens relationships even further. The only end to this is a happy one.

11

Intuition and Communication
A Winning Combination

By Donna C. Daigle
C-IQ Certified Coach | IOC Fellow | Intuitive Coach |
Life Coach
Sumerduck, VA, USA

> "Crisis has a fierce beauty. The beauty is not always evident while we are in it, but often is most profound when we get to the other side." ~Donna Daigle

I was born intuitive. It showed up early and strong. In school, the most common notation on my papers was the comment "Show your work." Intuition was not appreciated in a learning system that trains cognitive thinking skills, especially in the fields of math and science! I pressed in and became almost obsessed with gaining knowledge. I cannot remember a time in my life when I was not enrolled in at least one class. With all the focus on learned knowledge and the fear of rejection for being "out there," I learned to ignore or stifle my intuition. Distrust became part of my internal conversation. This continued for years.

We can damage our health by the foods we eat and choices we

make, and in the same way, we can damage our intuitive abilities. Intuition diminishes when we live our lives in a way that is inconsistent with who we are. And it makes sense. If you are not living an authentic life, how can you connect to inner wisdom? You are at odds with yourself! Authentic living is full life integration. Inner trust is the foundation for personal development. This was the pivotal concept of my own Conversational Intelligence (C-IQ) journey!

Finding Yourself During Chaos

My studies had been widely varied and my career path reflected this. Through the years, I reinvented myself multiple times, searching for a career fit that was elusive. I landed in the field of radio and thought that perhaps I had found my calling. But what I finally realized I loved was the people I was impacting, bringing positive and encouraging thoughts to them each day. I loved the off-air phone calls with listeners. To hear what struggles they had and to let them know they were not alone was wonderful. But I wanted to be able to do more. I wanted to walk with them on their journeys. So back to school I went to become a coach.

With this shift in career paths, the internal noise was beginning to quiet. I was starting to have moments of intuitive response. I had pressed into mindfulness practices that I had let lapse and life was beginning to have a rhythm once again. I was working with young artists and musicians at that point, with the occasional small business requesting my services. I was content that I had found my calling. And I was still learning.

Part of my learning journey was motivated by a lifetime of small but annoying medical problems that no one seemed to be able to diagnose. My research led me to papers written on the connection between the gut and the brain, which in turn led me to research on neuroscience. It was in this pursuit that I stumbled upon Judith E.

Glaser. She was getting ready to release a new book, *Conversational Intelligence*. At the end of the webinar, there was a phone number listed. I called it right away, believing I would get some secretary at CreatingWE Institute. Much to my surprise, it was Judith's cell phone.

When she answered the phone, she invited me into a new world! With her curiosity, complete suspension of judgment, and affirming language, Judith E. Glaser accepted me as a peer in a world that had only offered me perceptions of inadequacy and disdain. Then to my surprise, she offered me a role in co-creating a certification program for her life's work. I was honored beyond words. We spoke several more times and I was looking forward to beginning the journey after the holidays.

Crisis has a fierce beauty. The beauty is not always evident while we are in it, but often is most profound when we get to the other side. So it is with caring for aging parents. I was in a "suddenly" moment. With dementia and a fall where my mother sustained a broken wrist and fractured neck, the level of care she needed was intense. I called Judith to let her know I would be unable to be a part of the certification co-creation group. I put my coaching career on hold to be the primary caretaker for my mother during the final year of her life. It was a decision I will never regret!

After her passing, I was exhausted, grieving, and ballooned to weigh over three hundred and twenty-five pounds. I received an invitation to be a part of the inaugural Conversational Intelligence certification for coaches, and I jumped on the opportunity. I knew that understanding the neuroscience behind what I was experiencing was fundamental to improving my situation.

Those first couple of months were brutal. I was in so much physical pain from a host of medical conditions including fibromyalgia, celiac disease, and osteoarthritis, among other ailments. Although no one knew this at the time, I did most of my classes from my bed.

The constant encouragement from my peers and the radical acceptance I experienced from Judith began a healing process for me. As the oxytocin levels increased during the classes, I regained my ability to think clearly. I realized, of course, that some of my issues were physical. I found a reliable physician who uncovered some of the root causes underlying the health difficulties I had had for a good part of my life.

Changing my eating habits based on a ketogenic diet and adding some supplements put me on a fast track to better health. By the time certification was over eight months later, I had lost ninety pounds and was off most of my prescription medication. Combining the HeartMath techniques for coherence between heart and mind, changing my internal conversations with C-IQ essentials, and focusing on nutrition that was right for my body created space for greater innovation and inspiration. I began to feel and see changes. Truly, it was the support within my peer group community that catalyzed progressive positive change.

Going against our intrinsic nature will often show up as stress and impact physical health such as added weight, enzyme imbalance, or gut bacteria havoc. It impacts emotions and feelings of self-worth. We find ourselves trapped in an energy drain and are immobilized to the point of inertia. Stress impacts cognitive abilities. After continually being flooded with cortisol-producing stressors, the ability to think clearly and reasonably is at a low point. Such levels of stress leave their mark on the spirit. When that happens, it seems impossible to find any spiritual connection at all. Connection with the divine, with nature, with beauty, with ourselves, or with the world is elusive, at best. The result being that we are unable to see beyond the problem we are in. Decisions are made from a sense of immediacy instead of allowing for reflection. Creativity evaporates. Each one of these perspectives puts life and sustainability in jeopardy. Finding a way out becomes urgent. Finding balance is essential.

Judith E. Glaser, my mentor and friend, showed me through her beautiful way of being open to every individual, that if we believe in the value of each person, we *must* believe in the value of ourselves first. Once we have reached this level of awareness, we can stand firm and help others pivot. This is a solid place of confidence.

> "How well people bounce back from mistakes depends on their beliefs about learning and intelligence. For individuals with a growth mindset, who believe intelligence develops through effort, mistakes are seen as opportunities to learn and improve. For individuals with a fixed mindset, who believe intelligence is a stable characteristic, mistakes indicate lack of ability." ~ Jason S. Moser, Ph.D., Professor of Neuroscience, University of Michigan [4]

For managers, it is key! Confidence in your ability to lead your team, confidence in your ability to make good decisions, and confidence that you have value as a person and within the corporate structure gives a solid foundation for building a culture of trust. If you trust yourself, you open space for others to both trust you and themselves. The confidence of the leader affects the entire team.

When confidence is low, a growth mindset is inhibited. Without a growth mindset, intrinsic motivation is low, self-protection is high, and the brain introduces bias.[5,6] Decision making is impacted and operating from a place of fear becomes likely. When the brain is in a fearful state (amygdala hijack), creativity diminishes, and potential solutions are missed. If leaders see fewer possibilities, so will teams. Trust erodes and engagement plummets.

So how do we build back the confidence needed to turn this pattern around?

Your Intuition Improves Confidence

One of the buzzwords in leadership recently has been intuitive. Intuitive means having the ability to understand or know something without any direct evidence or reasoning process.

The concept of intuition has been around for centuries. It has been studied by scientists and philosophers alike. While most people agree that there *is* such a phenomenon as intuition, its definition and its source has been widely debated. In fact, although there have been many studies attempted, very few have shown actual evidence. The researchers all agree that something exists, but they do not seem to be able to agree on what it is or why it works. This has changed over the past couple of decades.

A recent study shows that "we can use unconscious information in our body or brain to help guide us through life, to enable better decisions, faster decisions, and be more confident in the decisions we make."[1] In leadership, confidence is paramount. Some may call intuition a neuroscience-based understanding of the ability to use unconscious memory to make quick decisions. And others may say it is a deep connection with the universe. Whether it is science or spirit, what good is inner wisdom if we do not have the confidence to use it? And. how can we develop intuition, whatever it is?

As with most skills and abilities, intuition increases when we exercise it. Here are six simple steps that can grow your intuition:

1. I - Immerse yourself in data. You do not need to be in classes for your entire life to benefit from the patterns developed by increasing your data pool. Taking a deep dive into what you are deciding can lead to a broader understanding of the issue. With more data available, your mind has more combinations with which to play.

2. N - Name your problem. Define it. Clearly defining a problem often leads to a solution by the words we

choose. Play with different wording to define the problem until you have something very specific.

3. T - Think of every possible solution, even ones that seem silly, impractical, or too costly. Many times, by thinking of the impossible, the possible becomes visible.

4. U - Unimagine the problem. Pretend that the problem does not exist. See if you can come up with a solution based on a desire. Instead of "This bicycle has a flat tire" try "I would like a bicycle that works." A change in perspective can often uncork the genie in the bottle!

5. I - Invest time in mindfulness practice. By quieting our minds, we allow space for our intuition to come to the surface. Time in intensive thinking, followed by time to unwind, will often bring solutions to the surface.

6. T - Thank your intuition. Maintaining a sense of gratitude toward yourself will keep pathways open in your brain that can help you in the future. You are training your mind to want to solve problems because it likes the sense of gratitude, it enjoys being appreciated.

Balancing cognitive and intuitive skills has improved my own life. During the certification process for C-IQ, my peer coach asked me a simple question, "What would it look like if you lead from your heart instead of your head?" It was in that moment that I realized that good portion of me was missing from my life. Because I was so obsessed with the intellectual pursuits, I had completely stopped listening to my heart and my gut. This was my pivot point. Being part of a culture of trust provided both the opportunity and the safety to explore questions that were, admittedly, uncomfortable. It allowed for self-exploration, for imagining possibilities, and it allowed me to be seen, to become visible. I did not realize the full impact at that time, but in looking back, I can see that this was the moment I began moving in from the margins.

Creating a Culture of Trust

> "We should be thinking about how we cannot just focus on ourselves but focus on the whole ecosystem, and that's not a moral responsibility—that's good business."
> ~Withold Henisz, Professor of Management, The Wharton School, University of Pennsylvania

Creating an environment of trust like the one I experienced is not difficult. And it is good for the bottom line! When you have engaged teams, with balanced lives, many of the pain points managers face disappear; absenteeism is reduced, high turnover rates come down, job satisfaction increases, etc.

Companies that have adopted practices that include sustainability, humane treatment of workers, and an emphasis on addressing social issues are in a better position today than other companies facing the current crisis. The improved relationships with all their stakeholders are keeping their performance significantly higher than those companies who have not adopted such practices.[2]

Building a resilient organization begins with building a culture of trust. Trust creates an increase in oxytocin levels in the body. Paul Zak, a researcher, and professor at Clairmont University, has identified eight ways to increase the brain's release of oxytocin that are also building blocks of organizational trust.[3] He uses the acronym OXYTOCIN:

- **O**vation – Celebrate each other and each win. Do it publicly. Public accolades are more effective than private, and it gives inspiration to other team members.

- e**X**pectation - Set clear, challenging, and achievable goals. Give feedback at least weekly. Avoid setting up a competitive environment. It reduces generosity and cooperation, oxytocin-building emotions.

- **Y**ield – Yield can mean both ownership of results and making way for another. Both concepts are important here. Make sure team members have a say in how they go about their work. Don't micromanage. Make sure they have the resources and training. Give them ownership of their projects and reason to engage with colleagues.

- **T**ransfer – Transfer responsibility to people to choose which projects they work on. Autonomy is stress reducing.

- **O**penness - Transparent communication between leaders and staff promotes trust by reducing uncertainty. Fear grows in uncertainty. Openness stimulates engagement, bringing more voices into the conversation.

- **C**aring – A caring culture encourages building social relationships at work, which builds oxytocin.

- **I**nvest – Invest in personal as well as professional development. Personal growth is important in every aspect of life. Organizations that develop whole people are often high-performing organizations.

- **N**atural – Honesty and vulnerability are traits shown by leaders in organizations where there is high trust. Showing authentic interest in others increases trust and respect.

Each of these eight steps involves conversation. Intelligent conversation. Through the tools and techniques learned from Conversational Intelligence, creating a culture of trust and a balanced workplace is possible.

Much emphasis is placed on cognitive skills in business. However, living a happy and successful life is equally important and takes tuning into heart. Finding the unique voice or expression of a person's individual motivational DNA fosters greater satisfaction both personally and professionally. Whether you are a leader, manager of people, or parent, self-development comes before development of others.

I will leave you with a story of a young man who followed his intuition and used exceptional communication skills and changed a life.

This is the story of the teenage young man, Tom, and another young man, Rick, both freshmen in high school:

Rick was new to the neighborhood and Tom did not know him well. They did not have any classes together and Rick always seemed a little standoffish. One day, as they were getting off the school bus, Tom drops his books on the steps right in front of Rick and then immediately bends down to pick them up. Rick, not really paying attention, trips over Tom, causing him to land face-first on the pavement.

To Tom, it felt like Rick had just kicked him in the rear and Tom was mad! Everything was going wrong that day already and now this! Rick's response didn't help!

"Oh. Sorry," he said as he walked down the road toward his house. Tom had a choice right then: he could perceive that as a sarcastic remark and an intentional kick, or he could believe the best about Rick. Fortunately, Tom chose the latter. As he picked up his books, Tom hurried along to catch up with Rick.

"Hey, dude! Did you do that on purpose?"

"No. I said sorry," Rick replied in a monotone voice.

Tom ventured on, wanting assurance, "Are you okay? It's Rick, right?"

"Yeah, just having a tough day. I guess I wasn't paying attention. I didn't mean to trip over you. Are you okay?" Rick replied with a little more expression in his voice.

Tom laughed. "I'm fine. It's not the first time I've fallen out of the bus although it may have been the most epic!"

This time Rick smiled and said, "I'm glad you're not hurt!"

Tom then engaged Rick in conversation as they walked the rest of the way to his house. They exchanged phone numbers and made plans to shoot some hoops later that evening after dinner. That day a memorable friendship began, and Rick went on to become the class valedictorian.

Rick gave his graduation speech four years later. He recounted the day he first met Tom. Rick had recently moved into Tom's neighborhood with his mom and younger sister. His dad had been convicted of beating his mom and molesting his sister. To make it worse, his dad had committed suicide before they could get him to the jail. The move to the new town was hard on all of them and no one talked at his house anymore. He was having trouble making friends at school. That day, Rick had been writing his own suicide note and was rereading it as they were getting off the bus. That is why he had not seen Tom stop.

Tom's gesture of friendship at that moment reignited hope in Rick. Perhaps things could become better. He went home and burned the note. In his closing sentence, Rick looked straight at Tom, standing among the other graduates: "If you, Tom, had gotten on my case or, worse still, ignored me that day, I would not be standing here today."

Let that sink in a minute. Our choices to see the best in people may not always have that kind of dramatic ending, but you never know. One day a choice you make might save someone's life! Maybe even your own.

This is a true story. Though the names and the details have shifted a bit through the years, and it has become urban legend, the impact and implications remain the same: your next encounter with someone having an off day could be pivotal in their life! We get to choose what kind of home, workplace, community, and world we create every day. Choose to see the best in people. Respond to them with honor. Listen to what they are saying, not just to their words, but to their tone of voice and their body language. Listen to connect.

Often the first perspective that requires adjusting is our own. Changing perspective begins with creating a space where trust can grow. Conversational Intelligence provides the tools to build trust and impact your life, your family, your business, your community, and the world in a powerful way.

Change your conversations. Change the world!

References

1 - Lufityanto, G., Donkin, C., & Pearson, J. (2016). "Measuring Intuition: Non-conscious Emotional Information Boosts Decision Accuracy and Confidence." *Psychological Science*. doi: 10.1177/0956797616629403

2 - https://www.theatlantic.com/sponsored/kpmg-2020/what-companies-owe-us

3 - Zak, P. J. (2018). "The Neuroscience of High-Trust Organizations." *Consulting Psychology Journal: Practice and Research, 70*(1), 45–58. https://doi.org/10.1037/cpb0000076

4 - Moser, Jason S et al. "Mind Your Errors: Evidence for a Neural Mechanism Linking Growth Mindset to Adaptive Posterror Adjustments." *Psychological science* vol. 22,12 (2011): 1484-9. doi:10.1177/0956797611419520

5 – Ng, Betsy. "The Neuroscience of Growth Mindset and Intrinsic Motivation." *Brain sciences* vol. 8,2 20. 26 Jan. 2018, doi:10.3390/brainsci8020020

6 - Sarinopoulos, I et al. "Uncertainty During Anticipation Modulates Neural Responses to Aversion in Human Insula and Amygdala." *Cerebral cortex (New York, N.Y. : 1991)* vol. 20,4 (2010): 929-40. doi:10.1093/cercor/bhp155

12

Case Study: Building Trust and a "Power-With" Culture

By Linda Keller
Trainer and Coach for Leadership, Team Development,
and Cross-Cultural Communication
Herrenberg, Germany

> "Who would have thought that in sharing what she had learned in C-IQ, she would receive an opportunity to co-create, design, and hold a one-day workshop on building trust and flattening hierarchies with no fewer than thirty-two managers and four levels of management, so quickly?"
> ~Linda Keller

Michael spent his first one hundred days as the new chief information officer walking through the department, talking to his direct reports, listening to the way people were talking to one another, watching how they were interacting, discovering how decisions were being made, and checking the productivity and quality of the work they were doing. This wasn't his first position as an executive board member, and he had recently completed a successful national change project in his previous company. This time, however, it was a change project that would affect the company on a global scale; he would be working more internationally, and all international communication would be in English, not his native language.

Julie was a freelance cross-cultural business communications trainer and leadership coach who believed passionately in continuous personal development and had recently become certified in Conversational Intelligence (C-IQ). She was also a native speaker of English. Having already fulfilled several contracts, in various roles, in almost every business sector of the company over a span of nearly fifteen years, she knew the company well and was not surprised when she was called upon to become Michael's English sparring partner.

As she passed through the security gates and wound her way up the stairs to Michael's office on the top floor of the building, she could not help contemplating everything she had heard about his first one hundred days. She had been impressed with the way he had begun his journey at the company, but she didn't envy him for the job he had to do. He was stepping into the shoes of a paternal-like figure almost everybody in the department trusted, enjoyed working for, and whose memory they were still loyal to. On the other hand, she had heard rumours that not everyone liked the way Michael had spent his first months at the company and knew he had a challenging task ahead.

Building Rapport

She reached the top of the stairs and stopped to clear her head of all her thoughts before walking down the corridor to look for the door to his office. This was a company that still had a rather tall hierarchical structure, so she was surprised to find both the door to his PA's office and his own wide open. The PA welcomed her in a friendly fashion and ushered her into her boss's office. Julie entered Michael's office with open curiosity and found him working at his desk. She briefly glanced around the room, taking in the pictures on the walls and flowcharts on the whiteboards, and realized she would be dealing with a person who was visibly and actively working on building a global destination not only for himself, but also for his department and his company.

Michael looked up, saw her, got up off his chair, and gave her a confident smile. He offered her a seat at a small round table in the corner of the room, and they sat down to begin their first conversation. Julie was curious to get to know the person, find out as much as she could about his pains and his visions, his hopes and fears. She enjoyed the fact that he was willing to share them with her in an open, honest manner. She asked questions for which she had no answers and just listened to connect and understand—not to judge, or in any way reject or confirm what she heard.

The Pains

As they talked it transpired that despite his best intentions, the impact Michael's first one hundred days had were far from positive. He had unintentionally caused an atmosphere of fear and distrust. Motivation was low in a business sector that needed to be innovative, agile, serve the global enterprise, and implement far-reaching change. Employees were clinging to what they had before Michael joined the company, and in spite of several attempts in workshops with various coaches and consultants to build trust, nothing seemed to be working. Other departments were beginning to notice the steady decline in productivity, too.

Michael had become exasperated and admitted, "Yes, there is a trust issue. I have done a lot to improve it and I keep telling them they can trust me." He showed her some slides and explained his own and others' efforts. He was frustrated with his staff and also with the state of the department. He thought he had too many managers who were only managing and not leading. Additionally, he had found the situation at the company, and especially in his department, to be a lot worse than he had anticipated.

Then, Julie felt her heart sink, as he told her he would soon have to take other measures, somehow "get rid" of some of his managers and replace them. He would bring in people he could trust and who, more importantly, trusted him.

Julie realized just how much TRUST really was an issue—not only did the managers not trust him, but did he even actually trust, and trust *in*, his managers? She asked him if they could just Double-click[1] on the word *TRUST* to see what he actually understood it to mean. He instantly liked the term *Double-click* and got the idea of what it meant immediately, so she went on to ask him to draw each "window" as it opened and fill it with that particular element of his understanding of trust as it arose.

With his own visual picture of all that trust entailed in front of him, she then asked him, to what extent he would say he trusted his team of managers. As he explained each element to her, he began to see his own role and behaviour from a balcony, from a very different perspective, a perspective he hadn't seen before. This simple exercise was starting to change his perception of the situation.

Julie seized the opportunity and quickly went over to the flip-chart, drew a long line with the words resist at one end, co-creation at the other end and in between those, doubt, wait and see and engage. She then asked him, on a scale of 1 to 5, 1 being resistance, 3 wait-and-see, and 5 co-create, where he would position himself on the line in connection with how well he thought he would be able to work together with the team as it was today.

1	2	3	4	5
Resist	Doubt	Wait-and-See	Engage	Co-create

He placed himself around 2. So, she asked him what it would take for him to move to 3, so to a wait-and-see mindset or even better, be prepared to move to 4, where he would be willing to engage, actively try a few more things out, and experiment. She explained her reason for asking was because 2 meant he was obviously doubtful, and with that kind of mindset he would be stuck, right here, in his primitive brain and put her hand just behind the lower part of her ear to signal where the primitive brain is positioned. She continued, saying what a pity that would be, because to be creative and come up with good, strong ideas on how to build and maintain high trust, they would need to work with the prefontal cortex, our executive brain, here, and this time placed her hand on her forehead to show where that part of the brain resides.

Going back to the flipchart, she now added the trust levels for each of the mindsets. Low trust, conditional trust, and high trust respectively.

The inextricable link between mindset and trust was now very visible and when she asked him where he honestly thought most managers in his team would place themselves on the line, he confessed, he thought a majority would probably be around 1 or 2, so in low trust in resist/doubt or at best wait-and-see mode, where trust would be conditional. This meant that neither he nor most of his team members were working with the full creative potential of their brains.

Julie asked him where they might place themselves if he told them he was contemplating a reshuffle and wanted to bring in some new external managers to lead the change project. But she needn't have asked—he had already begun to reflect his intentions and the impact they might have. His attitude softened as he continued to link his intentions with their impact, and his sensitivity to others grew.

In an open and trusting discussion, Julie shared parts of what she had learned during her certification course and since. How trust and distrust reside together in the brain, just in different parts, and how the part where distrust resides reacts more quickly. So, trust wasn't something that you built and would keep forever. It had to be fostered.

She shared what she knew of how the primitive part of the brain produces cortisol, how cortisol is linked to resistance, and how the effects of cortisol shut down other parts of the brain, making it almost impossible to access the executive brain. When cortisol abounds people mostly feel threatened, excluded, judged, and withhold information. How on the other hand, when the prefrontal cortex (the executive brain) opens and oxytocin, the "cuddle hormone" and neurotransmitter, abounds, people feel appreciated, creative, included, and share information; and how it is possible in conversations to Down-Regulate or Up-Regulate either cortisol or oxytocin.

"What if we could co-create a safe space for you to share this knowledge with your team and shift their mindset?" she heard herself say.

"Would you be able to do that for me in half a day?" he asked with an excited chuckle.

When she agreed, he quickly added, "And if we took a whole day, could we start changing the hierarchical mindset, too?"

It was Julie's turn to chuckle. Who would have thought that in sharing what she had learned in C-IQ, she would receive an opportunity to co-create, design, and hold a one-day workshop on building trust and flattening hierarchies with no fewer than thirty-two managers and four levels of management, so quickly?

The Action Plan

Thrilled at the idea of the challenge, Julie's creative mind began to bubble with excitement. She knew a workshop with thirty-two managers of four different levels might be a high call for one trainer/coach alone, so she suggested they co-create a road map of next steps to bring some clarity into the process before they parted. They took two colours, blue for what they would be doing together and green for what Julie would do on her own.

The road map was finished quickly and brought the clarity they needed to drive things forward. They arranged their next meeting in positive anticipation and said their goodbyes, grateful for the beginning of a new and promising working relationship.

Designing the Workshop

Julie went on to co-create the content together with Michael. He had used the time between their meetings to consider what he wanted to achieve and noted that she had not included the flattening of hierarchies in the title of their road map, which was very important to him. Julie asked if they could just Double-click on the words *flattening hierarchies* from his perspective and from his team's perspective. His intentions were to enable better, more open communication and so build trust.

After Double-Clicking, he recognized that the impact could, for some, be fear of losing power, and this would not build trust. Julie suggested that by making the workshop interactive and choosing activities that would work for every manager, at every level, paying great attention to the space they were creating, they could open up the hierarchy within the team without risking any element of fear.

They continued to Double-click on every bit of content they discussed to make sure they were both on the same page and never lost track of the main objectives: for everyone in the team to know each other better, trust each other more, have more transparency, and share a common goal.

When Michael told Julie that his deputy was retiring in four weeks' time, they agreed that the best time to have the workshop would be shortly after his successor arrived.

Julie knew it was vital to get off to a good start and that some people found it difficult to come up with ideas on the spur of the moment, so she decided to write to each of the participants in advance, introduce herself, and give them a small noncompetitive, personal task to prepare to share with the others during the workshop.

She took great care when choosing all the activities she would introduce in each phase of the workshop. She made herself aware of the intention she had for each one, and then looked at how she would feel if she were a first level manager, second level manager, third or fourth level manager. She wanted to make sure everyone was given a voice and each voice was heard. So, she set the room for small and whole group activities with tables of four that could easily be put together to make larger groups when required. She arranged to have one person from each management level at each table of four and started with groups that had not previously worked together.

At the end of the workshop all the managers would have openly shared ideas, co-created new opportunities, built new relationships, and strengthened old ones. They would have a common understanding and vision of shared success and know what their contribution would be to achieve that success. In addition, the new deputy would have found his place, and the team begun the shift from "power-over" to "power-with."

For Michael it would be a kind of new beginning. He had already decided he wanted to repeat the workshop in every country with every team he had and wanted Julie to do it with him. But that's another story.

References

Glaser, J. E. (2014). *Conversational Intelligence: How Great Leaders Build Trust and Get Extraordinary Results.* Brookline, MA: Bibliomotion, Inc.

[1] The term *Double-click* as used in the exercise was coined by Judith E. Glaser and documented in her book *Conversational Intelligence: How Great Leaders Build Trust and Get Extraordinary Results.* Brookline, MA: Bibliomotion, Inc

13

Stress Never Killed Anyone.
Did It?

By Marian Bourne
Stress Management | Health and Life Coach
London, United Kingdom

> "Conversations are not what we think they are."
> ~Judith E. Glaser

Stress has a significant impact on our health. Our bodies are de-signed with a set of responses that are automatically turned on to deal with stressful situations. It doesn't matter whether it's the pro-verbial sabre-tooth tiger or the boss from hell, the response from the body is the same. It's a very effective system for the short-term fight-or-flight responses we need when faced with immediate danger. Un-fortunately, our stress response in the twenty-first century is turned on too long and too often and, in the corporate environment, it is seldom turned off!

The likelihood is that there are stressful situations and stressful people every day. For those who have jumped on the familiar tread-mill of "working hard and earning money," who are far too busy for a holiday and if or when they do have time off, they take their work with them. In essence, they move their office to a better location for two weeks! Living like this isn't sustainable for health. The Japanese have a word *karoshi* that means "death caused by overwork." The medical diagnosis of karoshi is a stroke or heart attack.

The stress response can be turned on from the moment of waking in the morning to turning off the light at night. It can start commuting to work; listening to the news; arguing with a partner over breakfast; having a difficult conversation—with anyone!

The words we use and the words we hear carry nuance and power, they carry our intentions and they can easily be misunderstood.

"Conversations are not what we think they are," said the late ozJudith E. Glaser who developed and founded Conversational Intelligence, her life's work, to create within companies a foundation for trust and connection. At the heart of her work is the neuroscience of brain chemistry: understanding which kinds of conversations trigger our fight-or-flight response from the primitive brain and which nurture the higher brain activities of trust, empathy, and integrity. The right conversations drive positive change, transform cultures, and ultimately achieve outstanding results for every company willing to take a deep dive into the fundamental science of communication.

My own interest in Conversational Intelligence was the recognition that the primitive brain, when activated, would trigger a cascade of stress hormones—cortisol and adrenaline—and if activated often enough or long enough could cause inflammation. Inflammation often results in joint pain, gut problems, and a host of other physical symptoms, which, in most doctors' NHS surgeries in the UK are seldom recognised as being caused by stress.

Emotional stress is probably the type of stress that most of us can easily identify with.

And yet, paradoxically, it's emotional stress that is underestimated and overlooked: underestimated because most people living with high levels of stress have learnt to adapt and cope and overlooked because it's hard to recognise what the problem is when one is in the middle of it.

Additionally, for most people in a corporate environment, even if the problem is recognised, it's not easy to admit to feeling stressed and possibly not coping well. There could be repercussions—loss of a job.

Very often it's a simple "awareness" problem. We have all become so good at "getting on with it," we ignore the subtle messages of migraines, insomnia, weight gain, foggy thinking, and many more symptoms that demonstrate we are out of balance.

This was the case for Sally, age fifty-four, who was referred to me with exhaustion, hormone imbalances, and joint pain. When we first met, Sally told me she had a great life, she had sold her business, she had no money worries, and she had a great relationship. But something didn't feel right.

It was all true—the money, the relationship—but it turned out that five years before, when selling her business, she had been subjected to bullying and back-stabbing by people she had assumed would support her and had struggled to hold her life together.

Now, five years later, the lab results that measure adrenal function showed that her cortisol levels were out of the normal range and far too high. This meant that her nervous system was in the fight-or-flight response that results from stress.

How might stress be transmuted into illness? In his book *When The Body Says No*, Dr. Gabor Maté states that when emotions are suppressed, this inhibition disarms the body's defences against illness.

Long-term stress takes its toll on our health when what we are dealing with is unrelenting and unmanaged. It can be the big stressors like a death or a divorce, but it can also be the small things that accumulate and from which we don't easily recover.

We now know that our ability to handle stress and our capacity for the amount of stress we can handle can significantly depend on our traumatic experiences as children. This understanding has been highlighted in Bessel van der Kolk's book *The Body Keeps The Score* and by Dr. Gabor Maté in *When The Body Says No*. Both books refer to the Adverse Childhood Experiences questionnaire, which gives us important information to help evaluate whether childhood experiences may be impacting our present-day life and how we cope or don't cope.

When Sally was diagnosed with breast cancer shortly after we started working together, one of the first questions asked by her oncologist was "How much stress have you been under?"

Regardless of the type of stress or threat, our nervous systems are hard-wired to respond with cortisol or adrenaline and unless we are able to turn off the response in a timely way, the chances of getting a stress-related illness are increased. In an ideal world, our stress response is turned off the moment we are out of danger; typically, though, we seldom slow down or allow ourselves real time out, so the body seldom has an opportunity to turn off.

Not every disease, of course, is stress related. So, it's important to seek proper medical advice for any symptoms rather than believing they are "just" stress-related.

Stress and the relationship to illness is not a new phenomenon. Research goes back a hundred years and it appears that we each have a "preferred" system in the body that manifests our stress response physically. For example, the cardiovascular system, gastrointestinal system, or musculoskeletal system are common. Most of us know intuitively, the "preferred" way that our body lets us know we're not handling stress very well; migraines, high blood pressure, back and neck problems, constipation, diarrhoea are all typical responses. Almost every system in the body can be affected by stress.

How many CEOs, MDs, and senior executives do not take at least one of these: statins, aspirin, diuretics, beta blockers, ACE inhibitors? Usually, the wake-up call that someone might be suffering a stress-related illness is a visit to their doctor when "something doesn't feel right." It's not uncommon for a diagnosis of high blood pressure, high cholesterol, poor liver function, insulin resistance or a gut and digestive problem that appears to have arrived in the body "out of the blue." One day everything is fine, the next day there's a diagnosis that at best is the trigger for different lifestyle choices or at worst is a prescription for a lifetime of medication for a serious condition that comes as a shock because only last week everything was normal!

We don't become ill overnight; it doesn't arrive out of the blue. It takes time because we're hard-wired to adapt and heal. Since it takes time to become ill, there must be a point in time where we start to get symptoms that something is not quite right. I believe that we have forgotten how to listen to the messages our body gives us. We have lost the ability to tune in and notice our *distress response;* typically, the changes in muscle tension, heightened or collapsed breathing, postural changes or loss of concentration. And we don't pay attention to the little niggles, the aches and pains, the changes in our weight or changes in our sleep patterns that can be the first clues that our bodies are out of balance.

This was what had happened to Sally. Her story ended with chemotherapy and radiotherapy. And very importantly, she worked with a therapist on the emotions she had bottled up for so long.

Lifestyle choices and becoming aware of our somatic response to mental stress are key to understanding how to take care of our health. With awareness of our physical responses, we have a valuable barometer of how we react to stress and therefore how we can reduce our risk of becoming sick from stress. In effect, we build our immunity and resilience to stressful situations. Resilience means many things to many people but I like to define it as our ability to thrive in spite of the stresses that life throws at us or to put it another way, we can bounce back in spite of the stresses we have to cope with.

It's important to understand the connection between our thoughts, feelings, and our physical body; a good metaphor is that it is like a motorway with traffic going in both directions.

Thoughts and feelings can change our physical shape; how we move and use our body can change our thoughts and feelings. In case this concept seems difficult to grasp, it's good to remember times in our lives when we've been through a lot of stress; for anyone who has experienced the death of someone close to them for example, it's very clear that grieving and walking with a spring in their feet are not compatible. By comparison, think of falling in love and the energy and vibrancy that infuses every cell in the body!

Here's an Experiment You Can Try

Close your eyes and imagine the boss from hell. Allow yourself to feel the frustration, anger, hatred or whatever you feel and notice what happens in your body. Usually, there is tension or collapse; a constrictive feeling in the chest or a change in breathing or tightness in the gut—everyone has their own version of how their body responds to these sorts of situations. This very simple experiment is a great way to experience your own *distress response*.

Clearly, if our bodies respond to a thought, how might they respond to the words we hear? Why is it that it can be very difficult to let go of criticism or negative feedback? Our minds love pictures and so we create pictures from the words we hear, giving them meaning, importance, and power. No wonder they rattle around our head!

Luckily, there are usually a number of warning signs that help indicate when we're having trouble coping with stress. They fall into two broad categories of emotional and physical.

Emotionally we can experience a wide range of feelings and thoughts—anxiety, irritability, sadness, defensiveness, anger, mood swings, hypersensitivity, apathy, depression, feelings of helplessness or hopelessness, being trapped, bored, apathetic, having slowed thinking or fast-racing thoughts. The neuroscience about the effect of cortisol on the brain is now well established. Cortisol closes down our prefrontal cortex so we are less able to think rationally and make executive decisions; not what you want in a boardroom!

Physically it's very common to have any of the following: headaches, migraines, clenched jaws, chest pain, shortness of breath, pounding heart, muscle aches and pains, ulcers, indigestion, constipation or diarrhoea, increased perspiration, fatigue, insomnia, frequent colds from lowered immunity, or back problems including sciatica.

And then there are the more complicated symptoms like an increased use of alcohol, smoking, recreational drugs; physical and/or emotional fatigue, loss of libido, marital/relationship problems, or poor job performance.

All of the above can be felt or noticed if we are aware. But our stress physiology also affects us at an internal visceral and cellular level:

- Increased blood pressure
- Increased metabolism (e.g. faster heartbeat, faster respiration)
- Intestinal movement (digestion)
- Increase in immune and allergic responses
- Increased cholesterol and fatty acids in blood
- Localised inflammation (redness, swelling, heat and pain)
- Faster blood clotting
- High blood sugar that can lead to a diagnosis of being prediabetic
- Increased stomach acids

- Hormone changes affecting thyroid hormones and sex hormones such as oestrogen and testosterone leading to low libido
- Reduced production of collagen so a faster ageing process
- Loss of muscle mass
- Increased appetite for carbohydrates and sugar

So, the question we have to ask is, what can we do that will help prevent stress from making us ill?

There are no guarantees of course. Nothing in life is guaranteed. But our willingness to take action to prevent stress-related illnesses and possible burnout must surely be a better option than doing nothing.

Fundamentally, if we want to change our response to stress, we need to become aware of the mind/body connection and what we can do to bring about change.

Awareness is the starting point. Without being aware of the problem there can be no change.

A.W.A.R.E

Five simple steps I call A.W.A.R.E create strong foundations for effectively managing stress.

A   Assess

If we don't assess what the current situation is, there is no starting point. So the assessment must identify all areas of life that impact wellbeing, not only in the workplace but also lifestyle and social relationships. It's a subjective and quantitative evaluation using questionnaires and technological assessments that generate measurements that can be used to compare a stress management programme before and after.

W   Wake-Up

Gathering facts and data is useful but only if we can learn from it. We "wake-up" to our stress when we understand what our triggers are, what our default stress response is, and what the drivers are behind our responses. Stress usually affects particular systems in our body—back pain, gut problems, headaches, and migraines are typical somatic responses to stress.

The drivers are the beliefs we have that come from our childhood; very often they determine the levels of stress we can handle and the patterns of behaviour we use to cope.

A   Analyse

Choices always have consequences and the choices we make when we are stressed will inevitably not be made with our best thinking. Analysing the consequences and the choices we have made as a result of stress is important if only to show us that we need to change! Most people find it easier to move away from what they don't want rather than follow the path to what they do want. So analysing, recognizing, and owning our behaviours is the best way to motivate ourselves.

R   Reset

We can think of reset as rewiring our nervous system to achieve Mind-set Mastery. All our fight-or-flight reactions are driven by the sympathetic nervous system and the aim of learning how to respond in a different way from what we are used to is to lower our hyper-vigilance and sympathetic response and increase our parasympathetic response to keep us calm and balanced.

E   Embody

Nothing comes to us automatically if we haven't practiced new skills.

Roger Federer does not go onto centre court at Wimbledon to practice a new serve. He has practised and rehearsed it hundreds and thousands of times so that it is embedded and "wired" into his physiology and anatomy.

We, too, need to embody our new ways of being. There's an old saying in neuroscience "neurons that *fire together wire together.*" So we need to make our new responses to stress become second nature, much like learning to ride a bicycle or learning to swim. Once we have learned it, we can never unlearn it.

So, What Do We Need to Learn?

First of all, we need to understand that we can't eliminate stress. It isn't possible and the more we think life "should" be free of stress, the more stressed we feel. As the saying goes "what you resist persists."

So instead of thinking about eliminating or changing a current coping strategy, a better solution is to replace it with something more effective.

Broadly speaking, the following are recognised as very effective ways to lower the sympathetic response and increase the parasympathetic response.

- Breath work
- Muscle relaxation
- Meditation
- Visualisation
- Exercise
- Retraining the nervous system

Everyone is different so it's important to find what works and to have a few options to practice. Different stressful situations may require different strategies.

Stress does not discriminate; from the CEO down no one is immune and the effects can reach deep into a company, affecting its psyche and obviously the health of its staff. In an ideal world, planning and implementing programmes to deal with stress in the workplace needs to start at board level so that wellbeing is a priority for the whole organisation.

According to the WHO (World Health Organisation) working too hard is now recognised as an occupational phenomenon and it describes burnout as a syndrome that results from "chronic workplace stress that has not been successfully managed."

From experience, companies who organise educational talks or send emails to their staff about how to deal with stress, do not make deep, life-enhancing changes for their employees. All too often an educational talk is a series of slides that I liken to "death by Power-Point."

Learning how to change one's behaviours and thoughts has to be experiential. Whether learning to play golf or tennis, to meditate, to be a five-star chef or a top-class footballer, learning is always practise, practise, practise. And so it is with learning strategies to deal with stress. They need to be practised regularly to increase the chances of staying well and decrease the risks of becoming ill.

> "Set peace of mind as your highest goal and organise your life around it." ~ Brian Tracy

14

Case Study: Helping Clients' Dreams Come True with the C-IQ Toolbox

Eilish McKeown
MCC Coach| Career/Conflict Coach |Consultant CreatingWE Institute
Blackrock, County Louth, Ireland

> 'I am overcome with such pride and joy when I hear about the amazing things our graduates are doing with their C-IQ knowledge and tools. The work they are doing in the world is extraordinary. Here is a heartwarming story from Eilish McKeown on how her C-IQ tools led to one of her clients achieving their professional dreams."
> ~Judith E. Glaser, Thursday, 3 November 2016.

A young nurse called Laura contacted me to coach her for a very important interview she had coming up. The interview was to secure a training place on the National Public Health Nursing program at University College Dublin. Laura had already applied for this the previous year and was unsuccessful, increasing her determination yet also her anxiety about getting a role this year. By the time she had contacted me, Laura had already successfully completed the first stage of the application process and so was short-listed for the final interview stage—it was here that Laura sought my guidance to help her over the final and most crucial hurdle to secure one of those vacancies from a total of two hundred and eighty candidates.

Laura was referred to me by my sister who had told her about my work with C-IQ and the results my clients had gained from it (many of them also being successful interview candidates). We scheduled two three-hour appointments to get to work on preparation. When I first met Laura, she presented as a very bright, intelligent young lady. She described for me how the previous interview went for her, I teased out some of the issues, the questions, her responses, etc. She realized one answer in particular did not sit well with the interview board and described the feelings that created in her. We reflected on her learning from that. What I identified from my C-IQ tools was that the amygdala was triggered when she noticed her response was not the answer they were looking for (in my experience this is quite common at interview with candidates) and that set off a train of events.

Methodology Using C-IQ Tools

I decided to use primarily the Five Brains Model with Laura. I described the brain, how it works, showed her the diagram (from our C-IQ toolbox), and went through it—as she was from a medical background she was able to understand. I explained in simple terms that the amygdala was the oldest brain, when we are fearful it kicks in in a nanosecond, and if we don't recognize this it can take over and then our thinking brain shuts down. I explained how if she could learn to manage this at interview, and calm it down, she could have access to the whole of her brain, thinking, and knowledge to respond to questions. I talked about the new executive change brain, the neocortex library she could access for knowledge and of course the heart brain.

Then I focused on the interview board and how they have brains, too, and that she could actually control the interview through connecting with their executive brain, emotional brain etc. and how she might relate to them one at a time when being questioned. I suggested she make her answers interesting and tell a story to connect through conversation (C-IQ).

I believe the turning point for Laura was understanding if she could recognize the amygdala for what it is and calm it down then there would be no stopping her. I sent Laura off to read up on her answers and scheduled a second appointment. At the second appointment I rehearsed the interview with her approximately three times. I was amazed at how quickly she understood the C-IQ approach to conversation.

Outcome

Laura called me as soon as the interview was over—she was buzzing! She had stayed focused throughout and took charge of the areas of her brain where she stored all her knowledge and information, which essentially gave her confidence to respond. She saw the board members as real people interested in her. I know how sought after these posts are from my experience in health care so I was very excited a week later when Laura contacted me to say she was placed number twenty-four nationally on the panel and succeeded in getting one of the four jobs available in her local area. This meant she no longer had to do a two-hour round trip each day to work. A completely amazing result—I was stunned!

Laura started studying in University College Dublin on 5 September. I honestly put Laura's success down to the use of C-IQ tools (along with her enthusiasm to learn them) and of course her high level of awareness and intelligence. Laura's ability to hear and understand how we manage our brains in stressful situations led her to be calm, composed, and in control of the interview that ultimately led to her success.

This is a heartwarming, true account of a young girl with a dream to serve the community and now she is on her way to achieving it.

Laura's Conferring as a Public Health Nurse (PhN)

Laura, August 2017
Photo Credit: Niall McNally

Update on C-IQ testimonial from Laura, who in August of 2017 achieved her dream of being a Public Health Nurse.

I successfully completed the Public Health Nurse (PHN) course back in May 2017 and I had a beautiful baby boy in August 2017 (definitely my highlight of the year!). It was a busy year but I thoroughly enjoyed the course and the resulting job.

I had the pleasure of having a fantastic PHN mentor and overall team. I got great exposure to the different roles of a PHN and gained invaluable learning experiences.

I worked as a Community Registered General Nurse/PHN until my maternity leave began in August. I absolutely love my new role and the work involved. Every day is different, and no two clients are the same. I particularly enjoy the fact that I work with all age groups, from the elderly population right down the age groups to newborn babies. It's a privilege to have a job where people welcome you to their home as you care for their health needs.

Again, a huge thank you to you as all the above I put down to the result of your coaching using the C-IQ tools. It gave me a new confidence and self-belief that I could and would achieve my goal.

I remember very clearly driving to Dublin for my previous job but envisaging myself driving to a PHN role. Your advice on visualizing my dream and thinking positively about it was life changing. I'm forever in debt to you and your exceptional coaching skills.

15

Inclusion and the Brain

By Sonja Vlaar

Leadership and Organizational Development System
Coaching | Diversity & Inclusion
Boxtel, The Netherlands

> "If you happen to have a brain, then you are biased."
> ~ The NeuroLeadership Institute

Since the beginning of humankind, there has been the question of who is part of the group and who is not. It evokes something primal in us.

Although over thousands of centuries human beings have evolved and we are now in possession of a sophisticated brain with thinking capabilities, humankind's behaviour is still very much impacted by visceral bodily reactions.

Where do these inner reactions come from, what triggers them, how can we turn them into something positive, and what does this mean for the future of work?

I am fascinated by trying to find answers to these questions and would like to share some insights as to why inclusion is an important competency for everyone to master. We will look at inclusion through the lens of information processing, Conversational Intelligence, neuroscience, psychology, and cognitive behaviour.

Exclusion of Information

Research in neurophysiology, neuro-linguistic programming, cognitive psychology, and philosophy points to the central control in our brain that manages the inflow of information derived from our five senses.

Figure 1 shows how information flows from our five senses (touch, temperature, smell, vision and hearing) to our sensory organs and different types of memories.

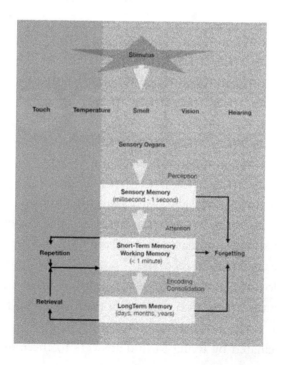

The inflow of information can be processed in many ways prior to storing or retrieving information from sensory memory: it can be ordered, categorized, and encoded.

During processing a lot of information is excluded. It is known that that the human body sends eleven million bits per second to the brain for processing, while the conscious mind seems to be able to process only fifty bits per second.

It appears that the vast majority of processing happens outside conscious notice and that most of the body's activities take place outside direct conscious control. This is the start of the creation of bias, what will be explained further in this article.

There are many physiological and biochemical reactions that are involved with the exclusion of information.

According to Amanda Blake, author of the book *Your Body is Your Brain* and thought leader at WBECS 2020, there are two modes, or circuits, of self-awareness that happens in anatomically different regions of the brain-body system. They are:

- Conceptual self-awareness involves face, head, neck, speech, and auditory centres in the brain. Conceptual awareness can bring you to any moment in time in the past, present, and future.
- Embodied self-awareness: an experience throughout the body, organs, and muscles, and areas in the brain. Embodied self-awareness is the *"felt sense"* knowing, an experience that only exists in the now.

The contemporary therapist and philosopher Eugene Gendlin originally developed the concept of the bodily *"felt sense."* He characterizes the concept as a combination of emotion, awareness, intuitiveness, and embodiment, and developed the methodology of *focusing*, which has similarities with methodologies of *mindfulness*.

The felt sense, according to Gendlin, is often unclear; people cannot specifically verbalize (yet) what exactly they are feeling, but often describe it as a vague awareness of things ranging from old psychological traumas to seeds for new ideas.

The felt sense is mostly present in the physical areas of the breathing: the stomach, the chest and the belly. When people have a felt sense, they are more in tune with their body. Focusing exercises can help them to shift the physical and emotional experience of the felt sense and consciously lean into other experiences.

Amanda Blake explains that the embodied self-awareness derives from combining three classes of perceptions:

- Exteroception: how we perceive the world outside our skin through stimuli from our five senses (touch, temperature, smell, vision, and hearing).
- Interoception: from stimuli from the body itself. We have thermoreceptors, mechanical receptors, and chemoreceptors in our nerve cells to sense temperature, pressure, and movement.
- Proprioception: from our ability to sense our body in space.

Each individual's brain-body system processes the inflow of information uniquely, perceives this information differently, and hence excludes different information.

John Mostyn Bowlby, a British developmental psychologist and psychiatrist, introduced the term "*defensive exclusion*" as different from other forms of exclusion of information. (Bowlby, *Attachment and Loss*, volume 3)

He explains that the difference lies not in the mechanism of information processing responsible for it, but in the nature of the information that is excluded.

Bowlby argues that the information likely to be defensively excluded is of a kind that, when accepted for processing in the past, has led the person concerned to suffer more or less severely. This means that unconsciously we exclude information to avoid suffering, to avoid emotional pain.

Bias and Social Exclusion

Due to the natural processes of defensive exclusion of information in our brain and body, we perceive the world through filtered information that create our biases.

Every individual has many biases. The bias has already started to produce thoughts in the brain before we are conscious of it in our thinking. Bias happens naturally to each human being. We cannot avoid it. The NeuroLeadership Institute postulates, "If you happen to have a brain, then you are biased." Humankind has biases built in.

In this article we dive deeper into a bias that hugely impacts our social interactions. This bias is the "affinity-bias" or the "similarity-bias"—the unconscious tendency to get along with other people who are like us, what gives rise to in-group and out-group dynamics:

- In-group dynamics: Perceiving people who are similar to you (in ethnicity, religion, socioeconomic status, profession, etc.) more positively. (*"We can trust her; her family lives near mine."*)
- Out-group dynamics: Perceiving people who are different from you more negatively. (*"We can't trust him; his family is not from here."*)

Biases are unconscious drivers and influencers of human behaviour. It is impossible to reduce being biased because bias occurs at the unconscious level.

Some people feel wrong when they discover that they have been biased, but this doesn't help. While we do not want to be biased, we cannot watch out for bias to happen, because the brain is wired in such a way that it will never be able to see that bias.

It depends on the context and the threat level that we experience if the bias will become visible in our behaviour.

While raising awareness with education so this can help people understand that they might be biased, standard skills-training about bias does not enable them to recognise bias in their own thinking and behaviour. The good news is that human bias can be mitigated with positive interaction and conversations that pay attention to information about our thoughts, reflection, and felt sense. We will present a methodology for such a conversation further in this article.

Social Exclusion Hurts

Joy Hirsch in her interview with Judith E. Glaser (YouTube, 2019) explains that the human brain in solo mode is very different from the human brain in interaction with others.

Social belonging is a fundamental human need, hardwired into our DNA.

As far as our brain's chemistry is concerned, feeling ostracized and excluded in a social situation is often experienced as real physical pain. (Eisenberger et al. 2003; Lieberman & Eisenberger, 2015). A brief experience of being rejected by someone we don't know can already make us feel sad and angry in a split second.

Memories of actual physical pain go away faster than memories of social pain. For example, if you stubbed your toe and it hurts, you can take an aspirin to get rid of the pain. But aspirin does not cure social pain.

Because the brain processes social pain differently, to relieve social pain requires narrative inquire and learning, as described later in this article.

Evidence in neuroscience suggests that the physical feeling of pain, for example from stubbing your toe, and the social/emotional feeling of pain from ostracism overlap in terms of how your brain processes it. That is to say, the same area of the brain that we know to be involved in processing physically painful feelings—the dorsal anterior cingulate cortex—is also relatively active when people feel excluded.

Even more than feeling these negative emotions, though, feeling left out disturbs the fundamental psychological need of all human beings, the need to belong.

Managers exclude employees more often then they themselves realise.

For example, a manager may argue, "I do not know why that person feels excluded, because I did not talk to him." The intention might be positive, but the effect of the behaviour of not talking at all, or of talking *to* the employee instead of talking *with* the employee may be perceived by the receiver as discriminating or excluding.

Once we have a bad experience in the social interaction and begin to become distrustful of someone that notion becomes embedded in our brain and can be difficult to dislodge.

When the amygdala then goes into the overdrive, it activates the limbic area of the brain, which stores our old memories. Emotional threats then send us into states of fear.

Goleman's theory about the amygdala hijack (Goleman, D. *Emotional Intelligence*, 1996) fits perfectly with Judith E. Glaser's framework for social interaction and her model of the three levels of communication and the levels of oxytocin-cortisol (Judith E. Glaser, *Conversational Intelligence*, 2014).

The Ladder of Conclusions

To create awareness about the way we think and to tackle bias, Judith E. Glaser developed the "Ladder of Conclusions." We can use this model to objectively and systematically inquire about our logical thinking.

Figure 2: Ladder of conclusions (adapted from the work of Judith E. Glaser)

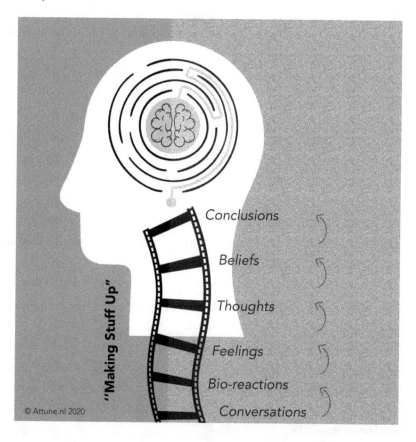

Walking the Ladder of Conclusions needs conscious effort because jumping to conclusions and being biased are part of our being human.

An Example:

I am standing in a circle with my European C-IQ Collective peers. We are engaged in a lively discussion about the redesign of the C-IQ tools into a new model with proxy-indicators for the measurement of primal visceral bodily reactions.

One of us, Cynthia, took the lead in the conversation with much enthusiasm, wildly cascading ideas with intensity and self-absorption, and not allowing space for any of us to break into her story.

Without awareness I took a few steps backwards. I stepped out of the circle.

Reflecting in the moment, it seemed that my body needed space. I was thinking I could not be near her.

I was thinking stupid thoughts. My rapid thoughts concluded:

- Cynthia didn't find it necessary to ask for my or others' ideas
- Cynthia neglected me
- Cynthia stole my ideas
- Cynthia might indeed find her ideas better than mine, she might be eager to apply the tool with her clients, or she might think I am too shy or afraid to embarrass her.

I took a deep breath and then joined the group again. But in the equation, something had happened; I felt excluded.

This all went very fast. In no more than a split second, I had climbed what Judith E. Glaser calls the Ladder of Conclusions, a common mental pathway of increasing abstraction, leading to misguided beliefs.

It started with the bio-reactions in my body, next I felt "not seen" and was convinced of "being excluded." With my thoughts and biased beliefs, I made stuff up, to conclude that Cynthia had excluded me and wanted my idea all for herself.

This all seems so reasonable and it happens so quickly, that—at that moment—I was not even aware I had climbed the ladder. All the upper rungs of the ladder took place in my brain. The only behaviour visible to anyone else was that—within one minute—I had stepped out of the circle and then stepped back into the circle.

The more I believed that Cynthia stole my idea, the more I reinforced my own behaviour of excluding myself from the equation.

I imagine there could be a counterpart reflexive loop in Cynthia's mind: as she reacted to my stepping back, she may have jumped up some rungs of her own ladder, too.

As every brain is unique, everybody has to deal with his or her own personal biases. That night I went over my thoughts. I realized that over such a small issue we could have found ourselves becoming enemies. I also recognized a pattern in my behaviour as I had leapt up that ladder many times before in similar situations.

The next day I raised the issue and we had a good conversation about what had happened, stepping down the ladder together. Trust was re-established, and from there we worked together to create shared success: a new tool developed by the European C-IQ Collective.

Bias is the shortcut our brain takes to make snap judgments before we realise that we are misunderstanding other people.

When we then climb the Ladder of Conclusions, we judge other people without looking at the real criteria of that person.

Human thinking normally and automatically starts with the conclusions that we want to believe; from there the conceptual awareness in our brain works backwards to construct a rationale that fits that particular conclusion. In that process we reject information that does not add to our internal coherence of what we already know and thus we provide ourselves with organizational defensive routines and a *"self-sealing logic"* (Self-sealing logic is a term coined by Chris Argyris in several of his publications.)

Unconscious bias leads not only to exclusion of information, it often also leads to social exclusion of persons. This social exclusion creates pain in the brain. Often, while already feeling the pain, one does not yet realize what bias makes them feel socially excluded.

How to Mitigate Bias?

Other people spot our biases better than we can.

Bias cannot be avoided but can be mitigated by having open-minded and courageous conversations with others. Using others as sounding boards can deepen our reflection and ownership of our behaviour and biases.

We can only grasp our personal bias when we are confronted with our or another's bias in expressed thoughts and feelings. Therefore we need to have conversational relations with people and have a dialogue to become aware of our biases, even when these conversations might become clumsy and uncomfortable.

Conversational Intelligence can be used to listen well, understand, and take the right perspective. The only way getting through bias is having intentional conversations that unfold the story we unconsciously made up for ourselves when we climbed the ladder and become aware of how we made stuff up. It requires working at the "being" level as well as the "doing" level.

From this awareness we can reverse the process and use the Ladder of Conclusions to reflect on each rung of the ladder, as we walk back down the ladder.

C-IQ Steps for Stepping Down the Ladder

Prepare: Set up time to discuss the situation/story in private. Be clear on your desired outcome and on your intention. Anticipate the impact it will have. Practice with someone (peer coaching).

Step 1: Connect. Set the context by saying you want to "process" the situation together so that you are more able to have a healthy conversation about something that happened in the past. Let the person know that you want to end up with a stronger relationship.

Step 2: Share stories: each person takes a turn sharing his/her reactions to and stories about the situation (facts, feelings, thoughts, beliefs, and conclusions). Listen without judgment.

Step 3: Discover impact: discover the impact the situation has on each other.

Step 4: Discover ripple effect: discover the effect it has on others.

Step 5: Attune: discuss how, in the future, you can do things differently, what actions and commitments you can make with each other for a better outcome. Agree to touch base, to get on the same page, and give each other feedback to ensure you achieve your desired outcome.

Intentional Inclusion as a Leadership-Competence

The impact of bias in teams and organizations is huge. The emotional connection that people have with their colleagues influences the extent as to which people are willing to demonstrate high levels of commitment and contribution.

Data shows that organisations increasingly recognise the value of diversity and having diverse teams. It is important to realise that no other person and organisation culture is better or worse than our own culture.

Other persons and cultures are just different, and increasingly we live in a world that is full of people that are culturally different from ours.

At the same time there is little awareness and reflection in organisations about the neuroscience of inclusion and its impact on engagement and performance of individuals and teams.

A leader might maximize diversity by asking different types of stakeholders to join at the table. However, being intentionally inclusive means that the leader goes beyond and encourages all voices to be heard, leveraging the unique qualities of each individual sitting at the table and inviting each of them to speak up.

The Women Innovators & Leaders Network (WILD) defines these concepts:

- Diversity: the presence of differences that make each person unique and can be used to differentiate groups and people from one another.
- Inclusion: valuing all individuals, respecting their differences, and supporting their development, which leads to engagement and drives business results.
- Engagement: the emotional connection people have with the company that influences the extent to which they are willing to demonstrate consistently high levels of commitment and contribution.

If people learn about their own biases in conversations with others and take the time to reflect together how bias causes misunderstandings or distrust, they can develop the competency of intentional inclusion and hence support the organisation in service of a sense of belonging for all.

For leaders it is a challenge to stretch and develop the competency of navigating conversations in a way that ingroup-outgroup is mitigated. Leaders can learn and develop the competence of intentional inclusion by navigating conversations more effectively, as well developing and role-model conversational language to become more alert to the advantages of equity, diversity and inclusion.

Individuals and teams with a mindset of inclusion create engagement, are more resilient, and perform better. Leaders in organisations have a responsibility to engage with their peers and colleagues and to reflect upon their own biases to be a role model for inclusion and engagement in their organisation.

Developing the competency of inclusion, by training both listening and uniting and creating awareness of the impact of biases, is a leadership skill that benefits the whole organization.

Summary

Intentional inclusion is such an important skill for every person—and especially for leaders—to develop in order to mitigate the impact of biases.

This is explored with findings of neuroscientific research about exclusion of information in the brain and body, the pain that is evoked by social exclusion and the self-sealing logic of biases.

An example is given how biases operate and how the tool of the C-IQ Ladder of Conclusions can be used to mitigate bias.

Human beings naturally and universally want to socially belong to others and need to feel being connected rather than experiencing the pain from exclusion.

But human brains are hardwired to exclude information and make us believe that culturally we are the normal ones and that the others are not.

To act inclusively we need to be conscious *and* intentional in our effort to improve social communication dynamics, be aware of the assumptions we make, and the stories we tell.

Because our brain is not hardwired for inclusion to automatically happen, the competency of inclusion needs to be learned actively and can only be developed in training the subskills of listening, understanding, and improving the interaction dynamics with others.

Therefore, intentional inclusion is a competency for everybody to develop. For leaders and organisations, it is important to facilitate learning processes for inclusion and engagement in their organisations.

16

In Memory of My Dearest Friend, Mentor, Colleague Judith E. Glaser

Eilish McKeown

MCC Coach| Career/Conflict Coach |Consultant CreatingWE Institute
Blackrock, County Louth, Ireland

> "I folded your clothes this morning...you weren't there."
> ~Richard Glaser in his opening eulogy for his wife, Judith

Working in the role of "Lead in Coaching & Mentoring in the Irish Health Service," I first heard Judith E. Glaser speak on the World Business and Executive Coach Summit (WBECS) webinar. I discovered this new body of information and signed up for the summit. It was 2014.

I listened to many speakers that summer and communicated with Ben Croft, WBECS's CEO, several times when my link to the online summit didn't work. To my surprise he called me at home to help with the connection. I remember thinking, "Wow, that is most unusual, to get this type of service." I felt such a part of something bigger in the coaching world. At the end of the summit we were asked to select our top speaker, and I submitted Judith E. Glaser as my top speaker for that year. (Second was Peter Hawkins whom I've met twice now and also admire his work in coaching.)

The rest is history. When Conversational Intelligence (C-IQ) was advertised with Ben and Judith, I knew I had to sign up. I registered for the Core & Enhanced programmes and paid a deposit to secure my place in the certification programme. Just before kick off on the 18 January, Ben sent an email to say something "sacred" would be shared at the launch, so I duly got out my three-candle set my deceased sister Bernadette gave me. I had them lit and ready to go. Judith shared that the 18 January 2016 was her wedding anniversary. I was gobsmacked when she told us that she had breast cancer fifteen years earlier and now has pancreatic cancer. My candles were shining in my window, the tide was in, everything looked normal, and when I shared this in the chat Ben and Lisa Knox (C-IQ program director at the time) said they had goose bumps. They did not know me at this point other than through online communications and emails.

I was present on all the modules live that year. I loved C-IQ, Judith, Lisa, and others on Judith's staff. Lisa hosted the meetings and she was a treasure: whatever you threw at her she came back with the answer in seconds. And Ben Croft was very visible making sure everything worked. In 2016 I so wanted to bring Judith to Ireland as I was vice president of ICF Ireland. My dear colleague Eoin McCabe was president and he fully supported this idea. I believed it was a great opportunity for the board members, Kathleen, Liz and James, and the ICF Ireland members.

In July of 2016, I travelled to New York with one of my sons Edward for the C-IQ graduation event. Those were the early days of C-IQ and the inaugural certification class of 2016. Everyone was buzzing; the event was outstanding like no other graduation I know. All C-IQ coaches were connecting at the most human level at the event and we had super food and beverages. Judith was in top form although she admitted to having "chemo legs" and asked our permission to rest them.

She engaged us in exercises around her experiences of developing C-IQ. One story she told was when she worked in an orphanage at age seventeen with young girls. The head teacher sent for her and Judith thought she was in trouble. It turns out all the grades had improved since her intervention and they wanted to understand what she did. She had listened to each pupil and created value and trust with each of them.

With Ben present and Judith signing her books, I recall thinking, "Now why didn't I bring my book?" only to remember I had a Kindle!!! So, I asked Ben, "Can I buy a book?" and he walked me straight over to Judith, picked up a new book, and asked her to dedicate it to me. I was chuffed and also struck by Ben's generosity. Ben later said to Edward he was grateful to me for my contribution to WBECS and C-IQ. While in New York I made the decision to sign up to pay for certification, which was my best decision. I stayed in the Waldorf and Edward and I went to dinner on top of the observatory at One World Trade Center; what a memorable time, meeting my heroes and celebrating with them.

I was keeping in touch with the lovely Lisa Knox, and Judith had a wee setback in the fall of that year, so we had to park the idea of her coming to Ireland.

I returned home and I kept in touch with Lisa who felt a trip to Ireland was now in the cards. I was excited. We began linking up in April of 2017. During this time, I had many Skype calls with Judith planning our event, some of these in the summer from my hotel room in Turkey. I hold wonderful memories of spending time planning the events with Judith. She shared some of her life with me and she called me her "master coach."

Back in Ireland Planning Judith's Events Commenced

In Ireland I set about organising events with the Health Service Executive. I travelled north to Belfast to meet with Ms. Diane Taylor from the National Health Service Northern Ireland (NHS) and the NHS signed up to host Judith in a workshop as part of their Leadership Programme. I also connected with Ms. Sinead Heneghan CEO of the Irish Institute of Training and Development (IITD) and they agreed to host an evening with Judith for their members. As the president of International Coach Federation (ICF) I arranged for a full day of learning for members and coaching colleagues from the European Mentoring and Coaching Council (EMCC) and the business world. All in all, we had six engagements and in this time, Judith would also be launching the 2017 C-IQ course from her hotel room on 11 September. I wondered what is it that gives Judith the strength to continue? I concluded it is her passion, developed in early childhood, for connection, teaching the world how to be conversationally intelligent.

Judith and Richard (her beloved husband) arrived on Irish soil on the 10 September 2017. When I went up to meet them early Monday, I was struck by how Richard took such good care of Judith. We taxied to our first event in the Kilmainham Hotel with IITD, where Judith hosted the afternoon session of C-IQ before the IITD event. We then had a break and on to dinner with the IITD where Judith was received with rapturous applause; this was to continue throughout our week together. Next day Judith was greeted by the ICF Ireland members at a full-day event in the Grande Hotel Malahide; many C-IQ coaches from the UK, Scotland, and parts of Europe attended. We had dinner in the evening with Judith, Richard, myself, and my supervision colleagues, Karen, Ailbhe, and Damiana. The conversation was electric.

Next evening Judith had a private engagement with very high-level businesspeople from Microsoft and other organisations. On Thursday she was the keynote speaker at the launch of the HSE Leadership Academy. We travelled onwards Thursday by train to Belfast to the NHS, who hosted a lovely dinner at Deanes at Queens. The next day we had a very full audience for Judith's half-day workshop. We managed to squeeze in a trip to the Titanic Quarter before catching the train back to Dublin. This was the end of a fabulous week for me of being in the presence of my GURU. I told Judith many times she is a GURU and it means "G you are U." Her humility was striking and of course Richard was minding us both.

When I dropped them off Judith asked, "So, what are we doing tomorrow?" I arranged a trip to Newgrange with one of my sons Edward as tour guide; he knows everything there is to know about Newgrange, a UNESCO world heritage site, so he agreed to be our tour guide and driver. Judith was so enchanted with Newgrange, as an archeologist herself it held great meaning for her. We have so many lovely photos of the visit, Judith filmed Edward and me, too. She had a great rapport with the tour guide as she understood so much of the detail of excavation etc.

So, on we went to Dublin where we visited Trinity College, which is amazing. Richard and Judith invited Edward and me to dinner, and I did some research with my ICF colleague James who recommended a beautiful restaurant. We had a most engaging conversation sharing food, wine, and breaking bread together.

Onwards to Malahide to their hotel, Judith asked Edward to assist her with something on her Twitter account, so we made it to their room. Honestly, it was such a rewarding day for me—we all connected in the most real, ordinary way.

Then Judith asked, "So, what are we doing Sunday?" Well, Edward was back to college, so I roped Colm, my husband, in as driver. We collected Richard and Judith and visited Kilmainham Gaol, as one of Judith's current nurses had family working there. We then walked around Dublin and visited Dublin Castle. As it was the All-Ireland Gaelic Football Final, the largest football event in all of Ireland, we found an Irish pub to watch the game and guess what? AIG, who is one of Judith's clients, was sponsoring Dublin, one of the teams in the final match. An amazing coincidence was that Judith was meeting AIG once back home on Tuesday in New York. She was so thrilled to be watching the final match, she took some video footage in the pub. Luckily, Dublin won, so it was a good news story for Judith and AIG. Following the match, we had some food together and then headed back to Malahide to the hotel. I said my goodbyes to Judith and Richard on Sunday night. What a privilege it was being able to share eight days with them.

Once home Judith continued to connect with me and we did this up until she passed away.

Back in New York

I had a call from Lisa in early 2018 asking me to participate in the Senior Dream Team as they felt I was "their rock" from the early days of C-IQ. I agreed and was really privileged to be a support to Judith the final day of her last appearance for C-IQ certification training, November 2018. Truth be told I fell apart with grief after this; I loved Judith, I could almost see her life purpose in her eyes, her heart's desire to having the world understand Conversational Intelligence.

I travelled to New York to her funeral and to say a final farewell. Ben Croft (CEO, WBECS) invited me to speak at the event he organised the day before, which was a privilege for me to share in the love of this great woman. On Sunday I attended the service with Lisa Knox, her mum, and Ute from the European C-IQ Collective. There were many C-IQ coaches there, including Lillian Cifrano Le Blanc, a dear friend who hosted Judith in Florida as I had done in Ireland.

Richard invited those present at Judith's memorial to his home, which was really nice. I love Richard, too. Richard and Judith were a most beautiful and handsome couple and it was clear to me he loved her very much. It was a privilege to be in her home and to see the artwork she and Richard created together. We shared stories with Judith's family of our warm experiences of her and visited the room where Judith first piloted C-IQ. On one wall of this special room there is a beautiful tapestry of that work. I began to think back to what it must have been like at the beginning, when Judith and a small team began putting together her life's work.

The eulogy included the voices of her brother, her daughter, her friends, Richard, and Ben Croft. It was strange being there without the lovely Judith. I will always remember Richard's starting line in his very short eulogy of her; he said that what he was about to read was a mix of things…songs and lines he found meaningful, some he found on YouTube. What jumped out at me at the beginning, "I folded your clothes this morning…you weren't there."

The next morning, I parted with Lisa and Ute at Penn Station, New York unable to speak with the tears.

Emails from Judith

I wanted to share with the reader some beautiful emails dear Judith took the time to write me once home, following her trip to Ireland. It gives you an idea of who she was and how much she appreciated all that was done for her.

Once Judith passed, I went back over our correspondence and reflected how she made me feel. She had this ability to make you feel you were the most important person…living in the here and now.

"WE DID It!!!!! I felt the magic in every cell… And I want to write a story to add to my new book about why and how our trip to Ireland was so magical and

healing.

Can you both help me (Rosarii) with this? It would be adding some paragraphs from your voices—about how magical/ or healing the trip was. I remember specific moments that were extraordinarily power for me...

Eilish, so many moments of joy—like the visit to the five-thousand-year-old Neolithic site at Newgrange, with you and Edward... I loved watching how much you love Edward...your relationship with him inspired me so much...I would be so thrilled to have you in my new book! Or, how it felt being in a real Irish bar celebrating AIG's winning game! So many great moments to choose from, this trip changed my life!

Thank you both for your compassion and support...

Every once in a lifetime, experiences come along that turn out to be transformational. That's the best way to describe my trip with Rich to Ireland for a week visiting with coaches, leaders, and curious businesspeople who wanted to know about Conversational Intelligence. *I remember on the flight home pinching myself—saying, "Did this just happen to me?" And here's some of the reasons why.*

First, I think I lived in Ireland in another life. I felt like I had come home. Everywhere we went, the people felt like friends, colleagues, and partners. And I know it had a lot to do with Eilish McKeown, one of our incredible Conversational Intelligence *certified coaches and president of ICF Ireland, who set up the whole week of speaking engagements and workshops with only spaces in between them to rest—recover—and reflect on the power and curiosity in the conference rooms as we engaged with deep questions, provocative insights and enlightening "ahas."*

Over the course of a week I met with hundreds of the most fantastic ICF coaches in Ireland and saw the amazing potential for Conversational Intelligence *growing across Ireland and Europe with the help of my new Irish Partners. With deep gratitude, I thank Eilish who turned an email into a trip of a lifetime, and the camaraderie and learning that went far beyond my wildest imaginations.*

Eilish introduced me to Rosarii Mannion, national director of HR in the Irish Health Services (HSE) who gave me the chance to launch their spectacular The Compassionate and Effective Leader Making a Difference Program that will touch the lives of executives and many more citizens of Ireland. I was the keynote for this extraordinary launch! I was so inspired by their program—the amount of energy and organization that Rosarii put into launching the program in Ireland... The attendance was incredible, and the engagement and excitement was off the charts! and Diane Taylor & Paula O'Kelly, the principal consultants at NHS in Belfast, and her key associates—all extraordinary and memorable experiences.

Eilish, thank you from the bottom of my heart! (I do believe I lived in Ireland in another life!)

Judith

Judith E. Glaser
Photo Credit: Breege Cameron

The above picture was taken of Judith at the ICF Ireland event September of 2017 sent to Richard from Eilish. Here's his response...

Dear Eilish,

What a great picture. I told you that when I first saw her, I thought she was the most beautiful woman I had ever seen, and as your picture shows, she still is!

I have to say it again, thank you for everything. You and your family were wonderful, and we met a lot of them!

Hugs to you, miss you, no 8:30 a.m. phone call.

Rich

BIOGRAPHIES

Marian Bourne
BSc
http://www.marianbourn.com

Areas of Expertise: Stress Management, Chronic Health, Certified Senior Coach with IAPC & M, Certified in Conversational Intelligence®

Marian runs a private Health Mentoring and Stress Management Coaching Practice in London, helping highly successful women in leadership reduce their stress levels and enhance their well being. A rich background of specialist therapeutic modalities in healthcare, 20 years treating chronic health conditions, and stress management coaching, give her valuably distinct skills in preventing high performing women leaders from hitting burn-out. Marian says, "Women in leadership are exceptionally good at keeping commitments to other people but they're not so good at keeping a commitment to take care of themselves; their mental and physical health can deteriorate as a result."

Elix Cintron
MA, CPC

coachelix@gmail.com www.coachelix.com

Area of Expertise: Executive Coaching, Leadership Development, Successful Career Transitions, Entrepreneur Coaching, Career Acceleration

With nearly two decades of proven success as a professional executive coach, Elix is a nationally recognized authority on growth and leadership. Using profound development tools, powerful business strategies, and his own groundbreaking G.R.I.P. methodology, Elix provides driven professionals with the skills necessary to accelerate success and achieve excellence in business and life. He specializes in coaching highly talented and highly motivated leaders and executives, focusing on elevating leadership performance, ensuring focus and execution, and finding balance amongst meaningful pursuits. Elix brings unbiased objectivity, confidentiality, motivation, and actionable support. Elix coaches in both English and Spanish.

Donna Daigle
www.donnadaigle.com

Areas of Expertise: Creativity/Entertainment, Passion/Purpose, Family, Natural Healing, Leadership & Team Development, Restaurants

Donna is passionate about co-creating beauty from chaos. Understanding that intuition (unconscious intelligence) is as needed as cognition (conscious intelligence), she connects individuals, families, businesses, and organizations with the authentic positive expression of their unique nature. With a career path that has taken her from the world of IT into the worlds of theater, broadcast media, and coaching, she is committed to bringing out creativity, trust, passion, inspiration, and motivation. As a Certified Coach in seven coaching modalities, including Conversational Intelligence®, Donna holds space for the full integration of cognitive and intuitive capabilities.

Christian Delez
https://ch.linkedin.com/in/christiandelez

Areas of Expertise: Agile Project Leader, Coach, Facilitator

Christian Délez is passionate about team dynamics and culture design. Christian works in a big Swiss company (RUAG) where he implements future of work patterns for more wholeness, purpose and high performance. He loves trying new human interaction patterns to bring happiness for each individual in families, relationships and at work. Christian is a co-founder of the Greatness Guild, the Swiss Association for Responsive Organisations and Good Practice Group. Currently working at RUAG MRO International, Christian has over 20 years project and agile work experience in health care, telecommunications, and defense.

Ute Franzen-Waschke
MA (WBIS), PCC

http://www.discover-your-choices.de/en/the-coach.html

Areas of Expertise: Coaching across hierarchies, Virtual & f2f Facilitation, Workshop & Program Design

Ute holds a master's degree in Coaching and International Business Communication (WBIS). She works with individuals and teams on communication processes, relationship building and co-creating work environments for individuals and teams to thrive. Ute's clients span the automotive & insurance industries as well as the public sector, and start-ups. Ute also provides training for coaches in different coach certification programs, is a mentor listed in the ICF Mentor Coach Directory and is a senior Consultant at the CreatingWE Institute. Before Ute started her own business, she worked in multinationals in various roles for more than 15 years.

Linda Keller
lk@lk-lingo.com

Areas of Expertise: Leadership and Team Development, Transition Coaching, Cross-Cultural Business Communication, Life coaching

Linda's passion is enabling individuals and teams to unleash their full potential by becoming more self-aware of who they are, of how they communicate, and by mastering their relationships with others. When people communicate effectively, they not only achieve incredible results, they do so more quickly, have fun, build trust, and become more resilient. Her clients span the global automotive, IT, insurance and banking industries as well as public administration and higher education across Germany, the UK, China, Sweden and Croatia. She holds several coaching certifications including Conversational Intelligence® and is a university lecturer for Intercultural Communication and English.

Eilish Mc Keown

www.rockmountbusinesssolutions.com
https://www.linkedin.com/in/eilish-mc-keown-mcc-4a7a9a26

Areas of Expertise: MCC Coach (ICF), Mentor, Conflict Coach, Career & Executive Coach, Supervisor, BA Management Studies, Consultant CreatingWE Institute

Eilish has thirty years professional experience across the public, private and voluntary sectors. She has worked in multinationals in finance and was lead in developing the Coaching & Mentoring service in the Irish Health Service. She was President of ICF Ireland in 2017 during that time she brought the late Judith E. Glaser to Ireland to speak about Conversational Intelligence. She is a Performance Enhancing Career Coach with a particular emphasis on continuous improvement, strengthening leadership capability, role transition and conflict coaching. Her philosophy holds that "each of us has within us the resources and potential for self-understanding and change".

Vicky Miethe
vickymiethe.dk

Areas of Expertise: Transformative Leadership, Design & Facilitation, Team Development, Engagement & Motivation

Vicky helps leaders and teams go from dysfunctional to cohesive co-creating teams that actively engage in building a psychologically safe work-climate so people approach change with curiosity and openness rather than resistance and avoidance. As a result, teams start to resolve disagreements before they evolve into conflicts. Their communication becomes healthy and supportive, so the engagement stays high and they start utilizing all their potential. Vicky's clients span the public sectors, finance, trade, and production companies. In all sizes. She holds a degree in finance and psychotherapy, and more than eight different certifications in coaching and consultancy.

Grace Moniz
M.S., BCC
https://impactfulexecutives.com

Areas of Expertise: Executive Coaching, Design & Facilitation, Leadership & Team Development, Inner Change

Grace helps organizations grow their most important assets – their people. Leaders accelerate and sustain personal change while enhancing their capacity to positively impact their organizations. In her work with teams, Grace infuses fun so teams develop a *foundation of common understanding*™ to which to apply their natural gifts. As a result, teams build trust, stimulate alignment, fuel engagement, and unleash creativity. Her clients span the aerospace, healthcare, higher education, consumer products, and air transportation industries. Grace holds a Masters degree in Organizational Leadership and applies researched based methodologies to support her clients' growth.

Tanja Murphy-Ilibasic

t.murphy@ps-development.net

Areas of Expertise: Agile approaches at enterprise level, Project/Conflict Management, Facilitation, Virtual & f2f Content Design

Tanja has closely collaborated with major conglomerates for 25+ years as corporate coach and communications specialist. Her work focuses on how to trigger and drive lasting change within individuals, groups and organisations. Unlocking growth potential and enabling extraordinary levels of sustainable performance are key elements of this. Tanja has extensive experience in the pharmaceutical and petrochemical industries. She consults for several organisations, including the CreatingWe Institute and is both the initiator and current chair of the C-IQ EU Collective Association.

Karin Ovari

https://karinovari.com | https://www.linkedin.com/in/karinovari

Areas of Expertise: Behavioural Safety Leadership & Team Coaching & Development, Designer for the Future of Human Connection, Passion for Psychological Safety, In-Person Virtual Event & Workshop Designer and Facilitator

"The future of human connection is creating the space and conversations required for true collaboration. By blending the best of both analogue and digital, we can transform human connection for your world." Karin brings 30+ years' leadership experience in varioussized organisations and across multiple disciplines from co-leading expeditions in Antarctica, working on oil rigs, to training in the corporate IT world. As a global citizen living on her 5th continent, known as the Aussie in Scotland, she comes with a broad and deep understanding of people, behaviours, cultures and communication styles. Her coaching studies bring a lifetime of practice and theory to life.

Jane Owen

MSc, Women's Leadership & Transitions Coach
linkedin.com/in/jane-owen-8779582
Janeowen@blueyonder.co.uk

Areas of Expertise: Woman's Leadership, Role transition, Maternity, Career Strategy

Jane helps leaders solve their career challenges and gain the work-life-balance they desire for greater fulfillment at work and at home. Jane provides a safe space for her clients to explore their challenges, so they gain insights and most importantly build sustainable habits to achieve the results they want to make. Her clients span the private and public sectors. As a management consultant Jane has a deep understanding of what it takes to be successful in an organization from starting out through to preparing for a board role. Jane holds a Master's degree in Business Administration and multiple coaching certifications.

Carina Vinberg
PCC
https://www.linkedin.com/in/carina-vinberg-943aa440/
https://framgangare.se/en/home

Areas of Expertise: Leadership training, Value driven processes for higher Trust in Individuals, Teams and Organizations I Virtual & f2f Facilitation I

Generous, curious, and engaged, Carina has enormous energy and a strong focus. Her passion lies in helping clients identify their values and core competencies so they become clearer, more confident and credible as an individual and leader. Taking a neuroscience-based approach she contributes to trusting cultures with greater wellbeing, better cooperation and achievement. Carina triggers growth, innovation, awareness and practice through tools for successful self-leadership. With +15 years as self-employed coach she has worked with executives and top athletes. Her clients span the sectors of Investment, IT, Start-up, Insurance and Education at Sports Academy. Carina holds multiple Coaching Certifications."

Sonja Vlaar
sonja.vlaar@attune.nl

Areas of Expertise: Leadership and Organizational Development, System Coaching, Coach-Supervision, Diversity & Inclusion, Virtual & f2f Facilitation

Sonja empowers leaders and their teams to build deeply strong foundations to leverage Diversity & Inclusion, Resilience, Communications, and Trust, in themselves, their teams, families and communities. Sonja's clients span the public sectors, training and coaching companies, finance, and tech innovation companies. Prior to starting her own company in 2004 she worked with multi-stakeholder projects in international development cooperation. Sonja holds two Masters degrees (as a nutritionist and as a Coach-Supervisor). She is a multi-certified coach including Conversational Intelligence and Organization & Relationship Systems Coaching. She is a senior facilitator with WBECS, Ethical Coach and Women Innovators & Leaders Network.

Charlotte Weston-Horsmann

https://www.linkedin.com/in/charlotte-weston-horsmann-pcc-7b618349/

Areas of Expertise: Executive Coaching, Intercultural Communication Competence, Team Coaching, Leadership Development

With over 15 years' experience as an external coach in global organizations, Charlotte helps international professionals communicate effectively across cultures, develop leadership skills and situational communication agility. As a project manager in the non-profit sector with project sites situated in North Africa and the Middle East, she was instrumental in aligning international partners, project teams, and USAID toward a common purpose. After ICF certification, Charlotte shifted her focus to working with international executives and clinical study project teams in the pharmaceutical sector to coordinate collaboration. As a result of co-creative coaching partnerships, we continue to create team cultures of inclusivity.

CPSIA information can be obtained
at www.ICGtesting.com
Printed in the USA
FSHW020251190920
73455FS